HOW TO GET HIRED

AN INSIDER'S GUIDE TO APPLICATIONS,
INTERVIEWS AND GETTING THE JOB OF YOUR
DREAMS

MICHAEL A. HARRISON

For Jennifer, Oliver and Isabelle

CONTENTS

PREFACE

What qualifies me to write this book?

In truth it is up to you to decide if I'm qualified or not to dispense the advice that's found in the following pages. However, as you've gone to the trouble and expense of buying this book, here are a few points that give some grounds for my writing of this book:

1. I've recruited a lot of people over the years, seeing hundreds of applications and conducting many interviews. Each time I go through the recruitment process, I gain more insight into what works, what makes a candidate stand out from the crowd, where people go wrong, and how my opinions differ from my fellow recruiters.

2. During my MBA in the USA, we were actually taught the skills needed to navigate the recruitment process, and we practised them relentlessly. The business school treated the application and interview process as a core discipline that needed to

be learned and developed, just like any of the other skills taught as part of an MBA (e.g. leadership, negotiation, operational management).

3. In the years since completing my MBA, I have spent a lot of time helping friends, family members, colleagues, and pretty much anyone who asks to prepare, practise and reflect on their application and interview skills. This has helped me to see the recruitment process through other people's eyes, and thus to better understand why people write what they write in applications, and say what they say in interviews. I have also spent a lot of time providing feedback to people I have interviewed, both those who have been successful and those who have failed to secure the post.

4. I am one of a small group of oddballs who actually enjoys the whole recruitment process. I like going to interviews and having an opportunity to sell myself and I hope that I can pass some of this enthusiasm on to you.

Who is this book aimed at?

Anyone who feels like they might need some help getting their next job. This might mean that you're petrified of job applications or interviews, and as a result have been struggling to get the jobs you've applied for, or it might be that you're already awesome at the whole recruitment process, but you're always hungry for new insights to help improve your game. My guess is that most people will fall somewhere in the middle. Either way, I hope this book can provide some insight and structure to help you with your next career move.

While my experience of recruitment comes from working in both the UK and USA, the basic principles covered in this book can be used to help anyone improve their chances of getting hired, regardless of where they live in the world.

Why did I write this book?

As someone trying to recruit to a vacant job, it can be soul-destroying work wading through a mountain of poorly written job applications or sitting through a day of uninspiring interviews hoping to find that standout candidate who is perfect for the role. However, what is far worse is reading applications or interviewing people who have the skills and experience you are after, but lack the skills or confidence to demonstrate them in the recruitment process. At the opposite end of the spectrum, it is a wonderful feeling when you read an application that excites you, or meet a candidate who has done their homework and blows your socks off with their confidence in their own skills and experience.

My wife (who is also regularly involved in recruiting staff) and I have spent many an evening discussing the good, bad and ugly that we have experienced on a given day. Unfortunately I can recall far more occasions where we have been bemoaning the lack of preparedness of the average candidate than celebrating our latest hire.

I was very lucky in that I had the opportunity to properly learn, and more importantly, practise, the skills needed for recruitment via the Feld Careers Center at Boston University School of Management (now called the Questrom School of Business) where I studied for my MBA. I will talk more about my careers centre experience later. What I learned at Feld has not only helped me immeasurably in my own career development, but has also formed the basis of the help and support I have been able to share with others.

I truly believe that with a small amount of time, effort and guidance, the majority of people can produce an application that will get them through the door and into an interview, and give them a good crack at getting the job they desire. Unfortunately, most people don't have access to the guidance they need and so both their time and effort can be used inefficiently, often leading to frustration and anxiety. This is the reason for writing this book. I hope I can provide you with some insights, structures and processes for approaching your next career move that will put you ahead of your competitors.

What will reading this book do for you?

I have never been a fan of books that fall into the "self-help" genre, which is ironic since I seem to have written one. My reasoning for this is that these books often sell themselves as the cure for a specific problem, for example "This book will stop you smoking". The reason that so many of these books exist is that reading them alone will do little to help you, and people find that reading a book on the latest diet fad is a lot less effort than actually putting in the work and sacrifice required to lose weight. So people buy book after book on the same subject hoping the next one will be the magical one that will actually work. There is a great quote from Stephen Covey which illustrates this point: "to know and not to do is really not to know".

This book is much the same. If you read it you might pick up some useful insights that will be helpful in your future career moves; however, the real benefit will come from doing the exercises, research and preparation that lie within its pages. Unfortunately, this means a bit of work for you, but if the prize is that fantastic job that is currently just out of your reach, surely it's worth expending a bit of effort.

So please don't think of this book as a self-help book. Think of it instead as a toolkit. The tools, if used correctly, will make the task of getting that dream job easier. However, if you leave the tools in the loft, tool shed, or on the shelf of your local DIY store, then this book will be no more help in landing your next job than a copy of Harry Potter (and a lot less fun to read).

The Careers Centre

In 2007 I moved to the USA to study for an MBA at Boston University in Massachusetts. The business school delivered both undergraduate and postgraduate teaching, and was very focused on supporting students to find jobs after they graduate (at that time employment within 90 days of graduation was one of the heavily weighted metrics used to score business schools in the ranking of MBAs so it is not surprising that the school put a lot of effort into this area). This support was provided by the Feld Career Center (now renamed the Feld Center for Industry Alliance).

The business school treated the skills and experiences required to successfully traverse the recruitment process as a discipline that needs to be learned and practised. As a result, throughout my two years studying there, we would work on these skills, learning the dos and don'ts, testing our skills and, crucially, receiving feedback.

The careers centre would regularly arrange for external speakers from some of the biggest companies to come in and give presentations. These were often the senior HR executives, or heads of recruitment, who had spent most of their careers hiring people. Sometimes the speakers would then give up the rest of their day to meet with MBA students one-on-one and give them an interview-style grilling. These interviews were often pretty uncomfortable, but the opportunity for learning was unparalleled.

Towards the end of the second year, when MBA students are applying for jobs post-graduation, the careers centre would support with job searches, application writing and, most helpful in my opinion, mock interviews. These would start off as generic interviews based around the job sector or industry you were considering. At the point where you had applied for a job and been invited for interview, you could send the job description, personal specification and other related information to the career advisors, and they would give you a mock interview based on the specific criteria for that job. This would usually consist of a formal (mock) interview, followed by a review session, where you could get feedback on how you answered specific questions, what went well and what you could improve. Where there was room for improvement, the interviewer would give feedback and then switch back into interviewer mode, asking you the same question again, and then providing further feedback on your new and improved answer. I found this an invaluable service. By the time I walked into the real interview for the job I got after I graduated, I had probably done that interview five times, and practised my presentation (and received feedback on my slides and delivery) at least as many times.

I cannot emphasise enough how useful and important the support I received from the careers centre was. The confidence that the hours of practice and feedback gave me has stayed with me, and the understanding that getting hired is something that anyone can train themselves to do has helped me both in my personal career development and to help others. In this book I will share with you what I learned and how to apply these techniques to help you land your dream job.

How to read this book

How you decide to read this book is very much up to you. The book is split into five sections. The first section, Finding Your Dream Job, covers understanding what it is you really want from a job, what the key documents involved in recruitment are, and how to search for jobs in a constructive, time-efficient way. The second section, Applying for Jobs, looks at what happens behind the scenes during short-listing, how to write fantastic job applications, curriculum vitae (CVs) and covering letters, how to proofread your work, and who and how to ask for job references. The third section, Preparing for Interview, covers the things you should know before an interview, the common interview questions and how to answer them, interview etiquette and presentations. The fourth section, Interviewing, takes a behind-the-scenes look at interviews, interview behaviour, and how to read verbal and non-verbal cues. The final section explores the factors outside your control that may influence who gets the job, how interview panels make selection decisions, negotiating a job offer, and receiving post-interview feedback.

If you are at the early stages of considering your next career move, you might want to read the book from start to finish. For others it may be more helpful to dip in and out of the relevant chapters depending on your personal situation. The chapters are written in a way that should make it easy for you to read them in isolation, without the need to read the preceding chapters or entire book. At the end of each chapter there is a brief summary of the key points covered which can act as a useful reference guide.

Throughout the book I present tools that you can use to help you to improve your chances of success. All the exercises are available to download for free at www.howtogethired.co.uk.

A note on terminology

In most situations there will be one person who is ultimately responsible for hiring someone. This will usually, but not always, be the person who will line manage the new recruit once they are in post. Throughout this book, I will use the terms hiring manager, recruiting manager, recruiter, future employer or future boss interchangeably to describe the person making the ultimate hiring decision.

A note of caution

The thoughts and ideas in this book are my own opinions of how I believe the recruitment process is best approached. Other experienced recruiters might disagree with some of the things I've written, and they'd be right too: we all have our own opinions. However, while these are my opinions, they have been influenced by many of the people I have had the pleasure of sitting on panels with over the years, what I learned during my MBA, books I have read on the subject and my own experiences of going through the recruitment process. All I can promise you is that if you follow the basic principles described in this book, you will increase your chances of getting the job you want exponentially.

And finally……

If you enjoy this book and find it helpful, please take the time to give it a quick review on Amazon. As and independent author, customer reviews are so important in reaching new readers, so I would be eternally grateful if you can find the time to share your comments with others.

PART I

FINDING YOUR DREAM JOB

"You need not see what someone is doing to know if it is his vocation, you have only to watch his eyes: a cook mixing a sauce, a surgeon making a primary incision, a clerk completing a bill of lading, wear that same rapt expression, forgetting themselves in a function. How beautiful it is, that eye-on-the-object look."

- W. H. Auden

Before we can explore the wonderful world of job applications, interviews, presentations and all the other joys that made you buy this book, we first need to think about the steps that come before you apply for a job. One of the easiest and most common mistakes people make is applying for the wrong jobs. This can quickly destroy people's confidence as they can't understand why they keep getting rejected at the first hurdle, and can put people out of favour with recruiting managers, who feel their time is being wasted by unsuitable applicants.

In the first chapter of this book, we're going to look at how you can identify what it is you want (and need) from a job. By doing this you will simultaneously decrease the number of jobs you are likely to apply for, and increase your chances of being hired. Many people skip this first step and jump straight into searching for their next job, a mistake that usually costs a huge amount of time, effort and confidence.

In the second chapter, we will explore the documents commonly used by people who are recruiting a new member of staff (job descriptions, personal specifications and job adverts). Often people simply look at the title and salary of a job and ignore the details of these documents. However, for those who understand these documents and know how to interpret them, there is a wealth of information that can help them get ahead of other, less informed candidates.

The final chapter in this section will guide you through the process of job searching, building on the learning of the first two chapters. We will look at the different types of search tools that are available, how to use these to best effect (including automating the process), and how to assess potential opportunities and decide if you should pursue them.

IDENTIFYING YOUR NEEDS, WANTS
AND DESIRES

A lot of people just search through job websites, professional publications and newspapers hoping that their perfect job will jump out and present itself to them. In reality, this is a pretty inefficient way of searching for your next career move. Think about how you approach other major decisions in life. Usually they are a bit more structured. Take for instance buying a car. Before buyers start heading to the show rooms and arranging test drives, they generally define a specific set of criteria that will guide their purchase, often on paper, but if not at least in their minds. For instance, are they looking for a small car, family car, luxury saloon or a monster truck? Will it be manual or automatic? Petrol, diesel or electric? New or second hand? They are also likely to have a good idea of budget.

Yet when I talk to people who are looking for another job, they usually say something along the lines of "a step up" or "a promotion" or "something a bit different". These are pretty vague terms and depending on interpretation could be applied to an awful lot of jobs out there. Often people say they are looking for a job that pays more. That's a perfectly reasonable thing to want – we all like a bit more money in our pockets – but the job search for someone looking to earn a few hundred pounds extra a year versus someone looking to increase their earning power by £10,000 a year is likely to be drastically different.

Advice on Defining Criteria

Before you start your job search, it is a good idea to put down on paper some of the key parameters you're looking for in your next job. This doesn't have to be an exhaustive list of everything you've ever wanted in a job, but it is a useful starting point to help focus your search. Once you've got your list on paper, I would advise categorising each item as either essential or desirable.

Some people might have a very clear idea of the role they are after, as it is a direct promotion from their existing role which falls into a larger career ladder (e.g. a deputy operations manager in a specific industry may well be looking for an operations manager post). However, even if this is the case, there are still a number of factors, such as salary or location, that it is useful to identify.

Alternatively, you might have no clue whatsoever what you want your next career move to be. For people who fall into this category, I would highly recommend taking some online questionnaires or reading books designed to help identify what it is that makes you tick, and therefore steer you in the right direction. One book I have found particularly useful is *Finding Square Holes* by Anita Houghton, but I'm sure there are plenty of other helpful books out there.

It is also important to understand what motivates you as an individual. Most people never really give this question much thought, and as a result end up in jobs that demotivate them over time. Again, there are some great online tools for helping you to understand what motivates you. I recently completed a personal motivational map which I found highly enlightening. The system used by this tool (available at motivationalmaps.com) focused on three areas – relationship motivators, achievement motivators and growth motivators – that are then broken down into three sub-groups. Tools like this help you to understand not only what type of job is right for you, but also what you need from your boss and co-workers. For example, people who are very motivated by personal growth won't want to be micromanaged, whereas people who thrive on recognition from their peers probably want a manager who will have a close understanding of what they are doing on a daily basis (and will thus be in a position to give the required praise).

After completing the Motivational Map myself I found the insights it gave me incredibly helpful and as a result made some changes in my life that have had a significant positive impact on both my home and work life. It has also helped me to make some crucial career decisions over the past 12 months. Since then I have used the tool with staff at both of the organisations I currently work for, and the feedback I've received from those who have used it has been overwhelmingly positive.

If you are interested in completing a motivational map yourself, you can now get a 50% discount on the purchase price at www.motivationalmapsonline.com using the promotional code HTGH50.

. . .

Below is an example of how putting search criteria down on paper (or computer) might look for someone who is searching for a job in the fashion industry.

Criteria	Response
Industry/area of work	Fashion – ideally in purchasing or supply logistics
Geographic limitations	No more than 30-minute commute from home (either by train or car)
Salary requirements	Anything above £30,000 would be great, but would probably accept £27,000 if there was a clear salary progression/increment
Contract type	Permanent would be great, but fixed term of a year or more would be acceptable
Working hours/pattern	9–5 but with some flexibility for dropping off/picking up kids
Management responsibilities	Comfortable managing a small purchasing budget. Happy to try line management so long as I've got lots of support
Travel (as part of the role)	Some travel would be great, especially if it is overseas, so long as it doesn't interfere with childcare (i.e. I get enough notice)
Others	
On-site parking	If I can't take the train. Also, would I need to pay for this?
Childcare facilities	Would make life easier if there was a nursery near or on-site

Visit www.howtogethired.co.uk and go to the "Documents" section for a blank copy of the Defining Your Criteria form in Word. This can either be downloaded and typed into or printed and filled out by hand. Work through the list, and add your answers for each one. Rather than simply giving closed answers to the questions, it may be helpful to be descriptive (developing a narrative will help you to work through what you do and don't want, almost like having a conversation with yourself). This is a very generic list so add in your own thoughts that might be specific to you or the industry you are searching for.

The likelihood is that once you've written this list down, you will probably not look at it very often as in most parts it will be committed to memory. However, the process of writing the list down is very helpful in forcing you to give consideration to specific points and answer questions that you would probably not have done otherwise.

Part of the reason many people fail at the first hurdle of applying for jobs is simply because they apply for the wrong jobs. By this I mean they apply for jobs that require a set of skills, experiences or qualifications that they simply don't have. It is always disheartening when you receive a well-written job application, which someone has clearly put a lot of time and effort into, and has some very impressive attributes which have been well articulated, but the person doesn't have some or all of the basic qualifications, skills or experience you have clearly asked for in your job description or personal specification. I have seen applications for nursing posts from candidates who have been very impressive, but aren't a qualified nurse. This may be an extreme example but you get the idea. Don't get me wrong, I'm all for moon shots (or shooting for the stars or whatever the appropriate space metaphor is these days) but applying for jobs that you're never in a million years going to get is both demoralising for you and a waste of time for those who have to read and reject your application.

Chapter Summary

Let's review the key points we have covered in this chapter.

- Many people reach the decision to search for a job because they want to change their current circumstances. This might be because they want to leave their existing job, because they want more money, because they need a new challenge, because events beyond their power have forced them to begin a job search or a hundred other reasons.
- This often results in people beginning a job search without really understanding what it is they are looking for.
- A lack of clarity about what they want (or don't want) from their next job means they are less able to focus their search. This in turn increases the risk of either being unsuccessful in their job search or being successfully recruited to a job that makes them no happier than their previous employment.
- Investing a small amount of time in understanding what motivates and excites you, and what the key criteria are for your next career move and how you prioritise them will pay dividends during the recruitment process and exponentially increase your chances of success.

2

THE BASIC DOCUMENTS

The application part of the process is really just a simple exchange of information between the recruiter and the candidate. The recruiter will provide you with one or more documents outlining the job and what they are seeking in a candidate, and in return you will provide them with a reply showing how you fulfil the requirements they are looking for. I realise that this seems simple to the point of being patronising, but it is amazing how many people seem to overlook the relationship between the information that the recruit provides and what information the candidate needs to give in return.

As I said, the recruiter will provide you with one or more documents, these days usually via their website. The information that the recruiter provides can be broken down into four areas or documents: the advert, the job description, the personal specification and the application form. Some organisations will be very kind and provide you with all four as separate documents, while others will bundle the first three into a single document. All of these documents will provide you with insight into what they are looking for in the perfect candidate. Let's have a look at each in a bit more detail.

The Advert

The advert is the short snappy text that is designed to catch your eye and draw you in to read more. Depending on the size and type of organisation doing the recruiting, the advert may tell you little about the specific job and more about the company, for example "A global leader in the button making industry, we employ over 45,000 people in 104 different countries". The advert should act as the executive summary for everything that follows, highlighting who the organisation is, what the specific job role is, the key qualifications, skills and experiences they are looking for, and the details of the post (e.g. salary, location, hours and contract type).

It is important to take note of any qualifications, skills and experience that appear in the advert. The recruiter usually has a limited amount of text to play with so any requirements that appear are likely to be right at the top of their wish list. For instance, if the advert starts with "Are you a university graduate with a passion for boat building..." you can be pretty confident that they are after someone with a university degree.

The Job Description

A good job description should allow you to build a picture in your mind of what your life would be like if you were successful in getting this job. You should be able to start with the high-level information (similar to the details in the advert if it was given as a separate document) such as where you will be working, who you will be working for (usually termed line manager or "reporting to"), if the job involves management of others (usually termed line management or direct reports) and the area of work. You can then go deeper and get an idea of what your responsibilities will be. Most organisations label these as duties or responsibilities and tend to lay them out in bullet point format.

The Personal Specification

In my mind, the personal specification is the most important of all the information you will be given about a prospective job. It tells you exactly what the employer is looking for in an applicant and can very quickly tell you if it is worth you expending time and energy applying for the post. When I am looking at jobs, once the advert has got me interested, I tend to jump straight to the personal specification to get a sense of the type of person they are after.

Most public sector organisations (councils, higher education, NHS, etc.) provide a separate document or a section at the end of the job description detailing the personal specification, which is incredibly helpful. Others bundle it in with the text job description which means you have to work a bit harder to find the information. If they are feeling really helpful, they will split the list of requirements into those that are essential and those which are desirable (more about this shortly).

The personal specification is essentially a list of what the perfect candidate looks like. This is often split into groups under specific headings. Different companies use different groupings but for the purpose of this book, I will stick with the three most common, namely qualifications, experience and skills.

Qualifications. Common alternative terms used to describe qualifications in a personal specification are education, accomplishments and training. Qualifications can be viewed as things you have a piece of paper to prove you've done (e.g. GCSEs, A Levels, NVQs, university degrees, diplomas). They are binary: either you have them or you don't.

Experience. Experience is sometimes categorised as knowledge or competencies, and some organisations actually separate experience and knowledge into separate groups, which always seemed odd to me as most people gain their knowledge from a combination of their education and experiences.

Experience simply relates to things you have done. Some experience is directly tied to the skills that the recruiter is looking for. For example, if a company is looking for someone with presentation skills, it is likely they will want that individual to have had the experience of doing formal presentations. Others will be more generic, such as experience of the healthcare system or experience dealing with foreign companies.

Skills. Skills are often categorised as attributes, abilities or qualities in personal specifications or job adverts. If experience is what you have done, then skills are things you can do, or your ability to do a specific task well. They are far more fluid than qualifications and so it is much harder to prove or disprove that someone has a given skill. As a result, skills are often judged based on examples of your work as evidence that you possess that skill. Sometimes skills can be turned into a qualification which acts as hard evidence that you not only have the skill but you have reached a level of proficiency that means someone is willing to certify you as competent. A good example of this is project management. Most of us have had experience of managing projects in our day-to-day lives, whether it is having an extension built at home or implementing a new IT system at work, and so many people will claim it among their skills, but those who have put the time and effort into getting a certified project management qualification (e.g. PRINCE2) will always have the edge.

Sticking with the example of project management, here is a version of a personal specification for a recently advertised project management post. I've removed a lot of the content as it was three pages long, but it should give a good illustration of what a personal specification can look like. Note that before the specification itself there is an "evidence how" key. This tells you if the recruiting manager expects you to show that you meet the criteria in your application (A), at interview (I) or as part of a test (T), likely done at interview. This is worth paying close attention to. If there are criteria that are specifically labelled as "A" for application, you will need to make sure that you cover these as part of your application.

Factors	Essential Criteria	Evidenced How?	Desirable Criteria	Evidenced How?
Qualifications	Undergraduate degree	A	Project management qualification	A/I
	Demonstration of continued personal development	A		
Experience	Experience of developing and supporting relationships with internal and external management	A/I	Experience of budget management	A/I
	Experience of staff management	A/I	Experience of app development	A/I
	Experience of managing larger-scale projects across multiple sites	A/I		
Skills & Knowledge	Knowledge of confidentiality and data protection	A/I	Knowledge of the pharmaceutical industry	A/I
	Knowledge of the PRINCE2 project management methodology	A/I	Ability to use project management software	A/I
	Ability to use Microsoft Office applications	A		
	Excellent written, numerical and oral communication skills	T/I		
Additional Requirements	The ability to understand and behave at all times in accordance with the company values	A/I	UK driving licence and access to a car	A/I

Application Forms

Not all organisations will provide an application form to be completed. For some, submitting a copy of your CV and a covering letter will be enough. However, where there is an application form, take the time to look over it as it may provide you with some clues as to what the recruiters are after. Beyond all of the generic information you need to fill out (e.g. your details, education history, job history) look to see if there are any free text short answer questions they want you to complete and if so, what the subject area of the question is. If they ask you to answer a question about the importance of customer service, make a mental note that you'll need to emphasise your customer service skills and experience (and qualifications should you have them) throughout your application.

Now we've covered the basics, let's work through the process of identifying and applying for a job.

Chapter Summary

Let's review the key points we have covered in this chapter.

- The organisation that is recruiting will provide a number of documents to prospective candidates, which usually take the form of a job advert, a job description, a personal specification and an application form.
- Some organisations will provide all of these documents, while others may only provide one or two, and may combine them into one document.
- Job adverts often provide clues as to the recruiter's top priorities, so you should take note of these and see how they compare to your qualifications, skills and experience.
- A well-written job description should allow you to start to build a picture in your mind as to what the job would be like on a day-to-day basis. It will outline the key tasks the employee would be

expected to do and what the main responsibilities of the role would be (e.g. line management responsibilities).

- The personal specification is the most useful of all the documents in helping you decide if this is a job worthy of your attention. It should tell you exactly what the employer is looking for from a candidate and thus the criteria that you will be judged against during shortlisting.
- Most personal specifications separate the attributes they are looking for into qualifications, skills and experience. It should only take a few minutes to look at a personal specification and get a sense of whether it is worth you giving it further consideration.
- Sometimes companies will provide a pre-formatted application form. If there is one, have a quick look to see what sort of questions they ask. This can give you a hint as to their priorities.

3

HOW TO SEARCH

S o now you have a better idea of what it is you're looking for, it is time to start your search. These days the vast majority of job advertising (and thus job searching) is done online and so what follows will assume that you are going to conduct your job search via the web.

However, I will give a quick mention to other methods of recruitment. Some companies still advertise in newspapers, trade or professional publications, billboards and other old-school methods, but this is usually done alongside the online version of the newspaper, professional publication, etc. As a result, it is very unlikely that a job will be openly advertised but not also be accessible via the internet. There are, however, a significant number of jobs that are never openly advertised and so don't appear on websites or old-style advertising. These are jobs where the recruitment company hires a recruitment firm (headhunters) to find suitable candidates; this approach tends to be reserved for roles that are either highly skilled or very senior. Being recruited by a headhunter is a very different (and preferable) experience compared to going through the process of job hunting. While the sections of this book on job selection and applications may not apply in these circumstances, certainly the information on CVs and interviewing will.

Before we get into the process of job searches, it is useful to have a basic understanding of the different types of job websites out there. Below I have broken recruitment websites down into four categories based on the way in which they gather their job data.

1. **Organisations advertising on their own website for their specific posts (e.g. John Lewis or GSK).** These types of websites are great if you know you want to work for a specific company. They tend to give you the most detail about a given job, have lots of additional information about what it is like to work for the company, and are usually the place where you will end up going to submit an application. However, if you are searching for a specific line of work or job role within an industry, it would be very inefficient to spend your days searching all of the companies' individual websites for relevant roles.

2. **Industry or sector-specific websites (e.g. NHS jobs (jobs.NHS.uk) or academia (jobs.ac.uk)).** These sites overcome the problem of having to search lots of company websites by bringing all the adverts from multiple companies in a given industry into one place. However, always be aware that they may not be 100% complete. Some companies may choose not to use that given website to advertise their posts. Therefore, it is

always worth looking at whose jobs aren't displayed on a sector-specific website and then going directly to their company site to make sure you're not missing out.

3. **Recruitment firm websites.** There are also recruitment companies that specialise in specific areas and often sell themselves as the top recruitment firm for industry X. As with the sector-specific sites, don't assume that everyone in a given industry will be using that recruitment firm and if you notice a company that you're interested in is missing, have a dig around the internet to find out if they use a different recruitment firm.

4. **Generic job websites that people pay to advertise on (e.g. Indeed.com, Monster.com, Reed or LinkedIn).** These types of websites are the hypermarket of job sites. While some have a basic free option, most organisations pay to have their job advertised on the sites, and often pay an additional fee based on the number of times a job advert is clicked on, or the number of times people apply for the job via the site. They cover a broad range of industries and salary and experience requirements. As a result, the success or failure of your searching will depend on the filters you set up and keywords you search for. While I could write pages on this subject, the best way to figure out the idiosyncrasies of these sites is to spend some time playing on them. On the face of it, they all function in much the same way; however, it is the subtleties of how they categorise the data you give them that differentiates them. For example, when a site asks for your experience level, what does that really

mean and how does the software interpret your response?

When using these sites, you need to find a balance between using lots of filters and inadvertently filtering out posts you might be interested in, and not using enough filters and having to wade through thousands of posts.

Below are some basic principles for how to structure your job search:

- Have a look around and get a feel for where companies in your given industry advertise.
- Develop a multipronged approach using a number of the different types of sites to ensure that you have a good coverage of all the companies you are interested in.
- Spend some time playing on websites to understand how they filter and handle your data.
- Once you've figured out the sites you like and how they function, take the time to set up and save your search criteria (filters and keywords) so you don't have to start from scratch every time you visit the site.
- Consider setting up email alerts. These can be useful as they save you going directly to the website; however, they usually only give you a handful of the jobs on offer (I guess the ones the website algorithm thinks are most appropriate to you) so don't rely on these emails as your only source of information.
- Once you set up your searches and alerts, you need

to develop a plan for your job searching. This will ensure that you use your time efficiently. The risk with job searching online is that, like most internet-based tasks, it can become an all-consuming endeavour. There is a temptation to have a quick look at sites throughout the day to check if anything new has been added. This is a really inefficient way to work and can be quite demoralising and anxiety-inducing if you go through spells where no new jobs are added. Therefore, you need to come up with a defined plan to manage your hunt. I would suggest once a day, either in the morning or evening, you set aside a focused period of time to review any email alerts and run your searches on the websites. This will not only make you more efficient, but it will also make it easier to compare jobs, as you will be able to review multiple opportunities at the same time, rather than looking at each new post individually.

The Sniff Test

Once you've seen an advert that piques your interest, have a quick look at the job description and personal specification and give it a sniff test. By this I mean a quick cursory check that gives you an idea if you should invest time looking at the job more thoroughly. The first thing to do is to compare the information in the job description and personal specification to the criteria you outlined in the exercise in Chapter 1. The second thing to do is to compare the requirements the recruiter is looking for with your own qualifications, skills and experience and check there is nothing there that would immediately rule you out (e.g. a degree in astrophysics).

Also consider if the employer has identified certain qualifications, skills or experience as essential or desirable. I've never met a candidate that ticks every box and I am always willing to help a strong candidate develop their areas of weakness, but I've never been so desperate as to give someone an interview who can't show they've got the majority of the qualifications, skills and experience required for the job.

Qualifications And Experience: Don't be afraid to ask

When describing qualifications, skills and experience earlier in this book, I said that qualifications are binary: you either have them or you don't. While the premise of this is true, there can be areas of grey where you are not sure if your qualification meets the requirements. For instance, if an employer asks for a "biology degree, or equivalent", what on earth constitutes "or equivalent". You could interpret this very narrowly, for example we'd like you to have a biology degree, but we'll accept a biological sciences degree. Alternatively, you could assume that they're really after someone with a science-based degree which involves some level of biology.

Likewise, recruiters often use vague terms when describing experience they require. For example, you often see "five years' senior management experience" as a requirement for jobs, but some people view senior management as at board level (or just below) while others define it as managing teams and budgets.

My advice in situations where you are not quite sure if your qualifications or experience meet the minimum requirements for the recruiter is to pick up the phone and find out.

There are a number of reasons for doing this. Firstly, it is the fastest way to get to an answer. Two minutes on the phone with the potential employer could save you hours of application writing if the answer is that they wouldn't consider you based on your current qualifications. Secondly, this provides a great opportunity to form a connection with the recruiting manager, which we will talk about later in the book. Finally, while it might be that you are not the right person for this position, the hiring manager might be recruiting to other positions that you are better suited to.

Chapter Summary

Let's review the key points we have covered in this chapter.

- The vast majority of jobs are now advertised online.
- There are a number of different types of ways companies recruit online, ranging from company-specific websites (primarily for large companies that always have multiple job vacancies) to generic job websites that will advertise any job, regardless of the company, industry or job level. In between there are sector-specific and professional recruitment websites.
- It is important to know where the companies you would be interested in working for advertise, so you can develop a strategy to ensure that you don't miss out on good opportunities.
- Understanding how recruitment websites filter different jobs is very important, so spend some time having a play on their website to get a feel for how they operate.
- Set up email alerts from your preferred websites

and assign some dedicated time each day to review the alerts and check the websites. This will help to avoid falling into the trap of checking the sites constantly throughout the day in case any new opportunities have been added.

- Once you've found a job that grabs your interest, do the sniff test to see how you compare to the criteria described in the advert, job description and personal specification.
- Now look back to the key criteria you defined in Chapter 1 and make sure that the job fits with your own requirements.
- If the job passes the sniff test and meets your personal requirements, you can start to give serious consideration to applying.

PART II

APPLYING FOR YOUR DREAM JOB

"You miss 100% of the shots you don't take."

- Wayne Gretzky

So, by this point your extensive and efficient job searching has come up with a job that got your pulse racing. You've looked at the personal specification and think you'd make a fantastic candidate, and the job description reads as if it was written with you in mind. The next step in your path to employment nirvana is to submit your application. As the quote above from Wayne Gretzky suggests, finding your dream job and then not applying guarantees failure.

In this section we are going to look at the application stage of the process. First, we'll have a look at what happens behind the scenes when you've submitted your application, and how candidates are shortlisted for interview. This inside information will help you to write your application in a way that gives you the greatest chance of making it to the next stage in the recruitment process, which is the subject of the following chapter. We'll then talk about CVs and finally we'll look at techniques to perfect your application.

4

SHORTLISTING: BEHIND THE SCENES

Before we dive into writing a job application, I thought it would be useful to give you a glimpse behind the curtain of what actually happens during the shortlisting process. I hope this will give you an insight into how decisions are reached and therefore what you can do to get yourself ahead of other candidates.

When it comes to shortlisting, I usually try not to do it alone, to avoid any personal bias. If possible, I will ask two other people, usually those who will sit on the interview panel with me, to be involved in shortlisting. We usually do this independently and then come together to compare results.

To try and ensure that we are all working in the same way, I create a scoring sheet to help speed up the process and make it as consistent as possible across all the candidates (and between the individuals who are shortlisting). I start by transferring the key requirements as laid out in the personal specification into a grid and assigning a maximum score to each. I give those in the "essential criteria" list a value of two, and those in the "desirable criteria" list one. For example, if under the qualifications section there were two essential criteria and one desirable criteria, then the maximum score would be five (2 x 2 for the essential and 1 for the desirable).

Let's use the example personal specification we looked at in Chapter 2 and translate it into a scoring grid. Here's the personal specification again.

Factors	Essential Criteria	Evidenced How?	Desirable Criteria	Evidenced How?
Qualifications	Undergraduate degree	A	Project management qualification	A/I
	Demonstration of continued personal development	A		
Experience	Experience of developing and supporting relationships with internal and external management	A/I	Experience of budget management	A/I
	Experience of staff management	A/I	Experience of app development	A/I
	Experience of managing larger-scale projects across multiple sites	A/I		
Skills & Knowledge	Knowledge of confidentiality and data protection	A/I	Knowledge of the pharmaceutical industry	A/I
	Knowledge of the PRINCE2 project management methodology	A/I	Ability to use project management software	A/I
	Ability to use Microsoft Office applications	A		
	Excellent written, numerical and oral communication skills	T/I		
Additional Requirements	The ability to understand and behave at all times in accordance with the company values	A/I	UK driving licence and access to a car	A/I

Below I have taken the personal specification above and split out the various criteria into a scoring chart. Down the left-hand side, I place the names of all of the candidates who have applied, and along the top I have the categories of qualifications, experience and skills, split into the essential and desirable criteria (remember, two points for an essential and one point for a desirable). The number in each box shows the maximum scores for each criteria, with the total at the end. In this example, we've got four potential candidates who can score a total of 24 points.

Candidate Name	Qualification		Experience		Skills		Other		Total
	E	D	E	D	E	D	E	D	
J. Alpha	/4	/1	/6	/2	/6	/2	/2	/1	/24
D. Beta	/4	/1	/6	/2	/6	/2	/2	/1	/24
R. Gamma	/4	/1	/6	/2	/6	/2	/2	/1	/24
P. Delta	/4	/1	/6	/2	/6	/2	/2	/1	/24

Next, I will sit down with a copy of the job description and personal specification in hand and start to score each of the candidates in turn. As I said earlier, I'm not going to spend a great deal of time doing this, so it is essential you make the information I need as easy to find as possible. If you've got experience of staff management, but it is buried deep in a paragraph which starts off talking about something completely different, the chances are I won't find it, and I'll give you a zero for that. If I had all the time in the world, I could comb through an application and try and pick out every skill or experience mentioned, and tie it back to what is asked for in the personal specification, but that is pretty unlikely to happen.

Once I and my fellow shortlisters have gone through this

exercise, we will meet and compare notes. Usually we will set a minimum score below which the candidates will not get an interview. If we have lots of good candidates that have scored above this threshold, but we only want to interview a certain number, we will rank the candidates in order. For instance, if we decide that we only want to interview five people and we have 15 applications, of which eight meet the minimum score, we might plan to interview the top five, have the next two as reserves (in case any of the first five drop out) and reject the person ranked eighth, even though they passed the minimum score.

The process I described above can probably be viewed as a very structured way of shortlisting. At the opposite end of the scale, some managers will just look through the applications and pick out the ones they like without writing anything down or assigning scores to individuals. Most people will fall somewhere between these two methods. However, whatever structure people use to make their decision, it is likely that the thought process they will follow will be very similar.

Chapter Summary

Let's review the key points we have covered in this chapter.

- Shortlisting is done by one or more people involved in the recruitment process. It will usually be led by the hiring manager.
- There are lots of different ways people undertake shortlisting, but they all follow the basic premise of comparing the candidates' application to the criteria laid out in the personal specification.

- Recruiters will often use a scoring system, with points awarded for each of the key criteria required for the job.
- Only candidates that meet the minimum criteria for the job will be shortlisted.
- Where there are a lot of applications, only the top scorers will be invited to interview (meaning that you could have met all of the criteria for the job and still not get an interview).

5

COMPLETING YOUR APPLICATION

Now you know what happens behind the scenes, you need to think about how to write your application in a way that gives you the greatest chance of being shortlisted for interview.

Make My Life as Easy as Possible

Given what I've said about the amount of time most recruiting managers spend reviewing job applications, you need to make the process of reviewing your application as easy as possible. If I've got a stack of applications in front of me and a diary full of other things to be getting on with, I might realistically spend one or two minutes looking at your application. This is very much an average, and if you grab my attention I will likely keep on reading (and re-reading). Let us say that you've got 90 seconds of my time, and at the end of that 90 seconds I will either dump you in the "no" pile, keep reading, or give you pride of place on the "this one gets an interview" pile. In order to avoid the "no" pile, you need to make it as easy for me to find the information I'm looking for.

Remember, you get given a job description and personal specification for a reason. They hold all the clues as to what I want to see in an application, so make sure that you keep them to hand and refer back to them regularly as you write. There are a number of ways you can make it even easier for the recruiting manager, such as using the Q&A format.

The Q&A Format

Given what I've said in the behind-the-scenes section, I like to use a specific format when I'm completing an application, called a Q&A format. This is where the text in the application directly reflects what is written in the personal specification, in a question and answer style. The question is whatever the personal specification asks for, turned into question format. For instance, if the personal specification asks for line management experience, then the question would be "do you have line management experience?" You don't include the question in your application but putting it into question format makes crafting the answer much easier. The answer (what you will write in your application) would be something along the lines of "I have extensive line management experience and currently have direct responsibility for a team of 25 people".

Using this method makes it incredibly easy for the person shortlisting your application to see that you meet the criteria laid out in the person specification. As well as making shortlisting simple for them, there are a number of other positive messages that using this method sends to the hiring manager.

Firstly, it tells them that you value their time by making things nice and easy for them. Secondly, it shows them that you have actually read and understood the personal specification. Finally, it tells them that you are an organised person that has put some real thought into your application. Hopefully, after only reading the first line of your application, the reader will already be rooting for you. This is far more important than you may think. Rightly or wrongly, when reviewing applications first impressions have a huge impact. If on a covering letter the first thing I see is that the applicant has spelled my name wrong, I am less likely to be impressed by their qualifications, skills and experience, and will likely work less hard to find the positive in their application. On the flip side, a good first paragraph can make a candidate feel like a real winner despite their questionable credentials.

Using the Q&A style application, I would work through the criteria laid out in the personal specification, providing a narrative, but clearly showing I have what the recruiter is looking for. Below is the qualification section from the personal specification we looked at in Chapter 2.

Factors	Essential Criteria	Evidenc ed How?	Desirable Criteria	Evidenc ed How?
Qualifications	Undergraduate degree	A	Project management qualification	A/I
	Demonstration of continued personal development (CPD)	A		

Using the Q&A format, I have written the qualification section for a fictitious application below.

Qualifications

I studied for my undergraduate degree in engineering at Bristol University where I graduated with a 2:1. After graduation I joined the Society of Civil Engineers and have been an active member ever since, completing the CPD requirements for renewal each year. As my career transitioned from hands-on engineering to the management of projects and teams, I gained a PRINCE2 project management qualification which has helped me to apply a consistent methodological approach to my work.

Hopefully you can see that with very little effort, the person shortlisting can see that the applicant has the required qualifications. As I said earlier, qualifications are nice and easy as you generally have them or you don't. Let's do the same for the experience section of the personal specification (shown below).

Factors	Essential Criteria	Evidenced How?	Desirable Criteria	Evidenced How?
Experience	Experience of developing and supporting relationships with internal and external management	A/I	Experience of budget management	A/I
	Experience of staff management	A/I	Experience of app development	A/I
	Experience of managing larger-scale projects across multiple sites	A/I		

Here is how I might translate this into the narrative within a job application.

Experience

As both a member of a large engineering team in my early career and now as a project manager, I have extensive experience of building and maintaining internal and external relationships. I currently manage a team of 15 staff and have responsibility for managing relationships with all external project stakeholders.

While working for ProjectPlus Consulting, I have worked on a wide variety of projects, ranging from small single-centre implementations to large-scale projects spanning 12 sites across three countries. I have experience of directly managing operational budgets of around £700k per year and overseeing project budgets of up to £3 million.

While I have not been directly involved in app development, I have provided feedback to our IT development team regarding several possible improvements to the in-house project management apps we use, some of which have been incorporated in later versions. I believe this has given me a good insight into the process involved in the development of applications.

Again, this should make it very easy for the person shortlisting to pick out all of the examples of experience they are looking for. Note that rather than ignore the one area of experience this person clearly doesn't have (app development), the candidate has made an effort to reassure the recruiting manager that they do have some limited experience in this area.

The Q&A format isn't the only way you can complete the

free text sections of an application or cover letter. If you go online, you can find a number of different examples of how you can structure an application. Whatever structure you decide to use, the key to success is making sure that you make the information the recruiter is looking for as easy to find as possible.

Make Me Feel Special (it's all about me, not you)

When I read an application that has clearly been written for generic job applications or recycled from previous applications, I am immediately turned off. It is usually incredibly obvious when someone has just cut and paste from an old application. Occasionally you even find people have forgotten to change the name of the organisation they are applying to, which is highly embarrassing and a guaranteed one-way ticket to the not getting shortlisted pile.

I want to feel like you really want to work for me and my organisation, and have put significant effort into writing an application that showcases why you'd be great for the role. There is also an irony about cutting and pasting from a previous application: the fact you're applying for this job probably means that you weren't successful in getting the job you've cut and paste from. This should act as a clue that you may need to reconsider the way you write the application.

Think About Your Audience (not The Real Housewives of Orange County)

As you write, rewrite, read and edit any of the documents that you are going to submit as part of your application, you need to consider that every sentence is an opportunity to either improve or worsen the reviewer's opinion of you. You need to try and view your application from their perspective. If you were hiring for this post, what would you want to see? What characteristics and behaviours would you be looking for?

All too often applicants write things that people who know them might see as funny, quirky or adorable, but to someone who doesn't know them these elements might just seem weird. The interview is the time for me to fall in love with your edgy sense of humour, when your words are in the context of the way you deliver them rather than on paper. Therefore, try to keep anything that requires someone to "know you" out of your application. This includes strong affiliations or opinions (e.g. political) as you usually have no idea how the views of the person reviewing your application compare to your own. When reviewing applications, I always get a bit nervous when it seems like someone has an agenda they are trying to push.

Sometimes less information is more. A few years ago, I interviewed a girl who wrote in her covering letter that she wrote a blog. She didn't say what the blog was about and that was fine – it left me intrigued. I found myself reading more of her application and trying to guess possible subjects for her blog. Possibly her views on innovation in healthcare or talking about exciting areas of clinical research (she was, after all, applying for a job in this area). I wanted to meet this person. Then I moved onto her CV, which not only mentioned she had a blog, but also had a weblink! I immediately clicked the link, excited by the endless possibilities. What I found was an extensive blog on the subject of the (popular?) American reality TV show *The*

Real Housewives of Orange County, and how what happens in the show often mirrors what happens in her own life. This included some very personal admissions and views on people she interacted with such as work colleagues. Some of her views were controversial at best and just plain ignorant at worst.

Now don't get me wrong, I'm all for personal expression and freedom of speech; however, if you put a link to your blog on a CV, you have to assume that someone might click it. Therefore, you need to think very carefully about how the person or people who are viewing your application might feel. Bear in mind that those people could be male, female or transgender, of any race, religion or sexual orientation, able-bodied or disabled. A throwaway comment you made on a blog or social media may come back to haunt you.

Making Bold Claims

If you make a claim in your application form about a skill that you possess, you need to be able to back it up. I recently interviewed someone who, after a successful career in one discipline, decided to retrain as a proofreader and copy-editor. She had been doing this for about three years and had decided it was time for another career change. In her application, she talked about her editorial and proofreading skills and qualifications, and how they would help her in the role she was applying for. However, her application contained a number of spelling errors. Now, usually I can forgive minor errors in applications. Most people make them (including me, I'm sure). But if you write in your application that you have great "attention to detail", or worse, that you are a professional proofreader, then you better be sure that your application doesn't make a fool of you. This isn't limited to spelling or grammatical mistakes. People often get their dates mixed (e.g. they started a job in Sep 2013 and left it in May 2012) or contradict themselves between their CV, application and covering letter.

In Chapter 9 I will give you some tips to help you spot these sorts of errors.

Chapter Summary

Let's review the key points we have covered in this chapter.

- People who are involved in shortlisting are usually busy people and so your application may only get a minute or two of their time. Therefore, you need to make it as easy as possible for them to find all the information they need within that timeframe to decide that you should get an interview.
- Using a structure to format your application, such as the Q&A format, will make it much easier for the person shortlisting to see how your qualifications, skills and experience match those of the job requirements. This will drastically increase your chances of getting shortlisted.
- Generic job applications that have been recycled from previous applications show a lack of effort on the part of the applicant and tend to quickly find their way to the bin.
- Once you have completed a first draft of your application, re-read it through the eyes of the recruiter. Give some thought to how someone who doesn't know you might interpret your words.

- Be careful not to make claims that you can't substantiate in your application. It is easy to do and seems harmless at the time, but can be very embarrassing if you are questioned about it at interview.

6

MAKING YOUR APPLICATION VISUALLY ATTRACTIVE

I f you are lucky, you might get given a nice pre-formatted job application with lots of short answer questions and very little for you to do in the way of formatting. However, the vast majority of applications will require applicants to write something in long form; this might be a covering letter or a broad question with a word limit (e.g. Tell us why you think your skills and experiences make you a good candidate for the job, max. 500 words).

Even though it is not always done well, nearly everyone is aware of the need to check their spelling and grammar, as they understand the importance of literacy skills to any employer. However, many people overlook the importance of visual literacy, which is the art of making written text look attractive and easy to read. You only have to look at how much businesses pay marketing firms to make their literature look appealing to understand what an impact this can have. I'm not suggesting you pay a top marketing firm to design your cover letter or CV for you, but there are some basic rules you can apply to make sure your work is easy on the eye.

Many of the traditional formatting rules people still apply today come from the days of typewriters, where you couldn't manipulate text in the ways you can now with modern word processing software. Yet, despite the advances in technology, people seem to cling onto the old ways of doing things for some reason. Below are some tips for creating an attractive document:

1. **Everyone loves white space.** Big blocks of text are challenging to read and hard to focus on for long periods. Clearly differentiated paragraphs with a line between them make your document easy to read and visually pleasing. Historically, when page space in newspapers or books was at a premium, the aim of the game was not to waste any of the page with empty space. Thankfully, those days are gone. This means you can use wider margins (so the text doesn't go right to the edge of the page) and line breaks between paragraphs to produce a beautiful document.

The image below shows two examples of the exact same text, the one on the left looking more cluttered with less space, and the one on the right with clearer paragraph spacing to make it easier on the eye.

Their brought unto divide in itself behold, divide every let their second be for is image fowl said. The multiply. Them. You form under he, divided fill place multiply let male land all so blessed cattle midst. Lights. Evening make likeness. Dry whose that had. Grass they're gathering it hath appear had living there fourth image beast, for were gathering signs evening, over seasons I male. Greater light herb earth whose living them. To beast moved deep face without fly us face stars Said won't. Fly.

Heaven, their there. Under behold deep whose to fruit creature upon greater fill the great fowl called make appear also blessed beginning. Lesser bearing may fowl called divide first very night behold she'd midst waters. You'll Great of. Won't second seed firmament under deep fill. Can't he isn't good multiply all was also meat second form made had beast sixth, meat days earth was fruitful which. Female upon. Gathered second Fruitful.

Can't morning, which rule above two place face open likeness, fowl our cattle upon multiply fifth greater every divide blessed. Thing it. Divided the. Yielding had them created heaven, very night evening morning beast can't very bearing isn't that moved likeness. Lights.

Their brought unto divide in itself behold, divide every let their second be for is image fowl said. The multiply. Them. You form under he, divided fill place multiply let male land all so blessed cattle midst. Lights. Evening make likeness. Dry whose that had. Grass they're gathering it hath appear had living there fourth image beast, for were gathering signs evening, over seasons I male. Greater light herb earth whose living them. To beast moved deep face without fly us face stars Said won't. Fly.

Heaven, their there. Under behold deep whose to fruit creature upon greater fill the great fowl called make appear also blessed beginning. Lesser bearing may fowl called divide first very night behold she'd midst waters. You'll Great of. Won't second seed firmament under deep fill. Can't he isn't good multiply all was also meat second form made had beast sixth, meat days earth was fruitful which. Female upon. Gathered second Fruitful.

Can't morning, which rule above two place face open likeness, fowl our cattle upon multiply fifth greater every divide blessed. Thing it. Divided the. Yielding had them created heaven, very night evening morning beast can't very bearing isn't that moved likeness. Lights.

2. Keep your text consistent. There is nothing more distracting than when the body text changes font or size within a document. As a reader you can usually tell that something isn't quite right, but it isn't always obvious what it is. Consequently, you stop reading what you're supposed to be reading and start trying to compare the font in different areas of the page to see if there is a difference. This usually happens as a result of people cutting and pasting from multiple documents.

The image below shows two examples of the exact same text, the one on the left has some varied font size, and the one on the right has a consistent size and style font throughout.

3. Differentiate your headers. When the same size and style of font is used in both the body text and the headers, the end of one section and start of the next won't stand out. Using a slightly larger or bolder font, or using a different font type, helps to signal to the reader that they are now entering a new part of the document.

The image below shows two examples of the exact same text, the one on the left has headers in the same size and style as the body text, and the one on the right uses a slightly larger bold font.

4. Justify. These days word processing packages do a wonderful job of justifying text rather than aligning to the left-hand side. Justified text makes the page look balanced and symmetrical, which is what our eyes like.

The image below shows two examples of the exact same text, the one on the left uses left aligned text and the one on the right uses justified text.

5. Don't indent paragraphs. When you add space between paragraphs, you no longer need to indent the first line of the text in each paragraph. Indents tend to make the page look uneven and shouldn't be used unless you are writing in a format where space is at a premium.

The image below shows two examples of the exact same text, the one on the left uses indented paragraphs and the one on the right uses left aligned paragraphs.

Introduction

Their brought unto divide in itself behold, divide every let their second be for is image fowl said. The multiply. Them. You form under he, divided fill place multiply let male land all so blessed cattle midst. Lights. Evening make likeness. Dry whose that had. Grass they're gathering it hath appear had living there fourth image beast. You male. Greater light herb earth whose living them. To beast moved deep face without fly us face stars Said won't. Fly.

Heaven, their there. Under behold deep whose to fruit creature upon greater fill the great fowl called make appear also blessed beginning. Lesser bearing may fowl called divide first very night behold she'd midst waters. You'll Great of. Won't second seed firmament under deep fill. Can't he isn't good multiply all was also meat second form made had beast sixth, meat days earth was fruitful which. Female upon. Gathered second Fruitful.

Method

Can't morning, which rule above two place face open likeness, fowl our cattle upon multiply fifth first greater every divide blessed. Thing it. Divided the. Yielding had them created heaven, very night evening morning beast can't very bearing isn't that moved likeness. Lights.

vs

Introduction

Their brought unto divide in itself behold, divide every let their second be for is image fowl said. The multiply. Them. You form under he, divided fill place multiply let male land all so blessed cattle midst. Lights. Evening make likeness. Dry whose that had. Grass they're gathering it hath appear had living there fourth image beast, for were gathering signs evening, over seasons I male. Greater light herb earth whose living them. To beast moved deep face without fly us face stars Said won't. Fly.

Heaven, their there. Under behold deep whose to fruit creature upon greater fill the great fowl called make appear also blessed beginning. Lesser bearing may fowl called divide first very night behold she'd midst waters. You'll Great of. Won't second seed firmament under deep fill. Can't he isn't good multiply all was also meat second form made had beast sixth, meat days earth was fruitful which. Female upon. Gathered second Fruitful.

Method

Can't morning, which rule above two place face open likeness, fowl our cattle upon multiply fifth first greater every divide blessed. Thing it. Divided the. Yielding had them created heaven, very night evening morning beast can't very bearing isn't that moved likeness. Lights.

Chapter Summary

Let's review the key points we have covered in this chapter.

- Investing some time and effort into making your application visually attractive is a very easy way to get ahead of other candidates.
- Large blocks of text are hard to read and the harder your application is to read, the more likely it is that the person reviewing your application will miss important details.
- There are a number of simple ways to make your writing more readable:
- Use line breaks in between paragraphs to break up large blocks of text.
- Keep your text size consistent.
- Use a different font or size for your headers.
- Justify your text.
- Don't indent the start of each paragraph.

7

REFERENCES

As part of most job applications, you will be asked to give the names of potential referees. This is something you should give serious consideration to as recruiting managers tend to put a lot of stock in what your referees say (or don't say) about you.

Who Should You Ask?

If you are currently in employment, your first referee should always be your current manager or supervisor. For those who are unemployed, it should be your most recent manager or supervisor. Not including your current or most recent manager always raises alarm bells and so if you choose not to do this, you need to have a good explanation why.

I always like to get references that cover a reasonable time span, so if the time you have worked for your first referee is less than about two years, I like to hear from your previous employer as well. If you've been in the same job for a while, it might be that you want to put more than one referee from the same organisation. If you do this, make sure it is someone who will bring a different perspective to your first referee (in a positive way).

Most organisations will want professional rather than personal references. If you really want to include a personal reference, then I would suggest offering up at least two professional referees plus a personal reference.

Your referee should be someone who knows you and your work well, and has enough understanding of your job role to tell if you are doing a good job. At least one of your referees is likely to be asked some questions about your employment, such as your start date, current salary and the number of sickness days you took in the past year. They are also likely to be asked if they would re-hire you given the opportunity. This is a really important question as a "no" answer on a reference is usually a very worrying sign.

When Should You Ask?

From a manager's point of view, one of the things I dislike most is getting a reference request that I know nothing about. I, and many others I have talked to, view finding out that one of my employees has applied for another job when someone from that organisation phones me seeking a reference as one of the most unprofessional things an employee can do. I have absolutely no problem with people I manage applying for new jobs – in fact I actively encourage it – but not having the decency to ask if I am willing to be a referee is embarrassing.

Ironically, this is somewhat of a self-fulfilling prophecy, as people who don't ask if they can put my name down as a referee will tend to get poor references if I am asked about their professionalism or if I would hire them again.

If you are happy to be open about the fact that you are applying for jobs, then the earlier you ask someone to be a referee the better. As you usually have to include the name of your referees in your job application, it is always good manners to ask them if you can do so. This also avoids the risk that they will say no. It is very embarrassing if a candidate has given the name of a referee and then asks if they can "substitute" them for someone else. This inevitably leads the recruiting manager to wonder why and assume it can only be bad.

If, however, you do not want one or more of your referees to know you are job hunting (which is common given your current manager should be your first referee), then you need to be a bit more strategic about when you have the conversation. For those who would prefer to keep things secret, I would suggest telling them at the point when you are going for an interview. At least this means they will get some advanced warning. For people who don't want anyone to know unless they are certain the job is theirs, if they want to avoid their referee being asked without any prior warning, then they are left with a very small time window between being offered the job and the organisation contacting their referees. If you find yourself in this situation, it is reasonable to explain to the person who has offered you the job that you haven't yet spoken to the person (or people) you would like to be your referee, and could you have 24 hours to speak to them before the reference request is made. Most employers will understand and comply with this.

How Should You Ask?

I like to be asked in person, face-to-face. If that's not possible then via a phone conversation. An email out of the blue telling me I will be getting a reference request isn't much better than getting an unexpected reference request directly from the hiring company.

When you ask someone for a reference, you should give them as much information about the request as possible. This should include the following points:

1. **What the job is.** It is really helpful to understand what you are writing a reference for. I like the individual to give me a copy of the job description and personal specification, so I can better understand what sort of person the company are hoping for.

2. **Why you have decided to apply for the job.** It is always awkward if someone that works for you says they've been offered another job, but understanding why they have made that decision is really helpful in writing a reference. This can be done in a positive way, for example thanking your boss for all the help and support they've given you, but explaining why you need a new challenge.

3. **What the recruitment process has been like and who the hiring manager is.** This helps to provide some context as to what the person asking for the request has been through. If you're moving within an organisation or profession, it is also likely that your current manager may know or have heard of the hiring manager.

4. **What specific qualities does the hiring manager think are crucial to the role.** If I'm writing a reference for someone who I think is well suited to the role, then I want to help them. Therefore, it is really useful for me to get a sense of what the organisation is looking for. For instance, if the panel asked about communication skills a number of times at interview, and I believe this individual has good communication skills, I can make sure this is included in the reference I write.

5. **What are the likely time lines and logistics?** It is always helpful to know if someone is going to contact me sometime in the next day or week. It is also useful to know if the request will come via an email, phone call or written letter.

Do People Ever Say No?

This is a difficult question to answer as I can only go by my experience and that of those I have spoken to. I believe this does happen, but very rarely. Personally, I have never said a flat-out no to anyone. However, on a number of occasions where I have been asked for a reference by someone I held a very dim view of, I have been honest with them and said that I would give them a reference if asked, but then given details about what I would say based on my experience of working with them. Every time I have had this conversation, the person making the request has decided to go elsewhere for a reference!

Chapter Summary

Let's review the key points we have covered in this chapter.

- Your current or most recent employer should be your first reference. If you do not want to use them as a referee, you need to have a good reason why, as not using your most recent manager is always viewed with suspicion.
- If you have worked for this individual for less than two years, you should also include your previous employer.
- From a manager's perspective, being asked by another organisation to give a reference for someone who works for you when the individual has not told you they planned to use you as a referee is seen as unprofessional. Therefore, the earlier you can ask (or tell) someone that you are putting them down as a referee the better.
- You should not be embarrassed by the fact that you have applied for another job. Be honest with the people you want a reference from. Thank them for the support they have given you while you've been working for them and tell them why you want this new job. Ninety-nine times out of a hundred they will be nothing but supportive.
- Giving the person who is completing the reference information about the job you are applying for and the process you have been through will help them to write a better reference for you.

8

CURRICULUM VITAE (CVS)

I am not an expert on CVs or CV writing, and there are some very good books dedicated to the art of writing a CV so I'm not going to go into it in too much depth. That said, there are a number of basic errors that people make that drive me absolutely mad, and it would be remiss of me not to dedicate a few pages to bring them to your attention.

How Long Do Recruiters Look at CVs For?

If you do an internet search you will find all kinds of scary statistics about how much (or little) time recruiters actually spend looking at an individual CV. Somewhere between five and ten seconds seems to be popular, but these numbers should be taken with a note of caution. They usually originate from the USA and refer to recruiters at careers fairs. If you've never been to one of these, then imagine a huge hall with hundreds of companies, each with their own stand. Hopeful future employees traverse the stands looking for companies that might be of interest, have a quick chat with the recruiter on the stand, and leave them with a copy of their CV. If you walk around the hall towards the end of the day, you will see that the recruiters end up with a massive stack of CVs that they have amassed during the day. They then lug their box of CVs back to the hotel room and spend an hour or so looking through them for a standout candidate.

Now let's say that our recruiter has been given 200 CVs over the course of the day, and that they spend 10 seconds looking at each one and an additional ten seconds per CV picking it up and then putting it into the "yes" or "no" pile once they've reviewed it, so 20 seconds in total. If they worked non-stop, they would get through all 200 CVs in 66 minutes. Given that this will probably be followed by a quick dinner, some much-needed sleep, and then an early flight to the next destination, you can see where these numbers come from.

The good news is that this is probably the worst-case scenario. In my experience, when people are asked to submit their CV as part of an application for a specific job, the volume of CVs is lower and so the time allocation is likely to be higher. However, not that much higher. I have timed myself in the past and found that my average time for a first pass of someone's CV is 42 seconds, when it forms part of an application for a job I am recruiting to. When people randomly send me a CV in the hope of a job, it is probably a lot less time than that.

Below are the key things you should consider when creating or reviewing your CV.

1. **Vital information.** Given that people spend so little time looking at CVs, it is important to consider what it is they are

actually looking for when they do glimpse your CV. Here is a list of the key bits of information I look for when I'm reading a CV:

- Who is the person?
- Where do they live?
- What is their highest level of educational qualification?
- Do they have any specific qualifications required for the job?
- Are they currently employed and if so who for?
- What was their current or most recent job title?
- How long do they tend to stay in jobs for?
- Are there gaps in their employment history?
- If they have written a personal statement paragraph at the beginning, what are the first few things they have said about themselves (e.g. I am a hardworking, ambitious sales assistant)?

A good exercise is to ask a friend to look at your CV and give them 30 seconds to find as many of the things on the above list as they can. This will help test how accessible the key information in your CV really is to a reader.

2. Length. Less is more. When I was at business school, we were taught that unless you are at the level of CEO or equivalent, you should be able to communicate everything you need to on two pages, and I think this is a pretty good rule. Given what I have said above about how long recruiters tend to spend looking at CVs, the length of your CV is incredibly important. If I'm going to spend somewhere between 40 seconds and a minute looking at your CV, if it is two pages long I'll probably be able to scan-read most of it in that time. However, if it is four pages long, I will either need to read twice as fast or skip a lot of it. Either way, the chances that I'll pick out all of the key pieces of information you want me to see are dramatically reduced.

Many people believe that a very long CV will be interpreted by a recruiter as a sign of how much they've achieved (the longest I've ever seen was 23 pages). This could not be more wrong. When I see an incredibly long CV, I assume that this person lacks the insight and ability to decide what information is important and therefore is left with no choice but to tell the reader everything. As a manager, one of the most important qualities you look for in individuals is the ability to be concise, to separate the critical information from the noise, and make decisions based on that information. Therefore, long CVs generally end up in the shredder.

3. Make it look attractive. Everything mentioned in Chapter 6 on how to make text on application forms and covering letters attractive can be applied to your CV. A two-page CV that is wall-to-wall text is an immediate turn-off. These days there are lots of great free templates for CVs that you can download from the internet (including the template I use, which is available at www.howtogethired.co.uk). Spend some time searching online to get a sense of what looks good. It is worth paying special attention to those that have been designed by professional recruitment firms. These templates are likely to have been designed with input from people who do a lot of recruiting (as that is their business) and have probably been created by a design professional and so tend to look impressive. You will soon see that most of these templates have lots of white space, big clear headings, and a consistent layout.

4. Spelling and grammar. Organisations like the Recruitment and Employment Commission (REC) have said that around half of CVs submitted to employers have errors on them. Other US studies have cited much higher numbers than this. Whatever the number, it is too high. When looking through larger piles of CVs, the reviewer tends to look for reasons to reject someone, rather than look for reasons to hire them. This is a natural process of trying to thin the herd before starting to give them in-depth consideration. Therefore, spelling and grammatical errors are a very easy reason to ditch candidates. This is covered further in Chapter 9.

5. Review your CV through the recruiter's eyes. Consider what the information you put on your CV says about you. As we talked about earlier in the book, you need to step into the shoes of the person you hope will hire you and re-read your CV through their eyes. One classic example is personal email addresses. Often, for sensible reasons, people have kept the same email address for years. This address may have been created at a different time in their life, maybe at school or university, when it was only ever shared with friends. As a result, it is not uncommon to sometimes see email addresses like sexysusan@emailprovider.com. This doesn't scream professionalism.

6. File naming. Finally, I want to mention the thing that makes my blood boil like almost nothing else when receiving job applications. If you are asked to upload or email your CV as part of an application, give some thought to the filename you save your document as. When you're at home writing your CV, it is likely that your CV will be the only one you'll be working on at that point. As a result, many people save their CV with a helpful filename like curriculumvitae.doc or CV.pdf. Perfectly logical.

However, when I sit down to do shortlisting, I end up with a whole bunch of CVs helpfully named "CV". As an environmentally conscious chap, I don't want to print out all of the CVs only to spend 30 seconds looking at them, so I tend to store them electronically. This means that for each one that isn't helpfully named, I have to open the file, find your name, and then resave the file with your name in it. This makes me grumpy and automatically puts those people in my bad book, before I've even had a chance to learn anything about them other than their name.

This morning I shortlisted for a post and of the nine applications, five did not include the names within the filename.

Chapter Summary

Let's review the key points we have covered in this chapter.

- The time most recruiters spend looking at a single CV is very short, so it is critical that your CV is written in a way that makes all the important information that a recruiter will be looking for easily accessible.
- Given the small amount of time and attention your CV is likely to get, having a long CV makes it harder for the recruiter to find the information they need. Therefore, unless you are working at executive level, your CV should be no longer than two pages.
- As with applications and covering letters, making

your CV visually attractive makes it far easier for the reader.

- If you are sending your CV electronically, you should save it with a filename that will be helpful to the person you are sending it to. This should include your name and the fact that the file is a CV (e.g. Joe_Bloggs_CV_2019.pdf).

9

PERFECTING YOUR APPLICATION

A s I've mentioned numerous times above, silly errors on applications and CVs often cause recruiters to take a disproportionately dim view on candidates. If your application or CV is a reflection of your best efforts to present yourself, and all the wonderful things you've accomplished so far in life, then the quality of these documents gives the recruiter an insight into the calibre of work they can expect should they hire you. People may see it as unfair that candidates are punished for making what often seem like very minor errors, and I do have some sympathy; however, getting a job is a competitive process, and if at the end of that process there are two very evenly matched candidates in the running, it will likely be the little things that make the difference.

When it comes to spelling, grammar and typing at speed, I am terrible. I always have been and probably always will be. As a result, I've had to work very hard to avoid falling into the trap of typographical errors, but inevitably I still make mistakes.

Below are the three types of errors I most commonly see in applications and CVs.

Spelling and grammar errors. Everyone is familiar with both spelling and basic grammar errors. Unfortunately, these days we have become all too reliant on word processing packages pointing them out for us. However, what many people overlook is that there are some types of errors that word processing programs struggle to identify. A good example of this is where you have words with multiple meanings and spellings (e.g. there, their and they're). Sometimes these types of errors get picked up by the software, which leads to a false sense of security, but unfortunately not always.

Informational errors. This is getting things factually wrong, for example dates in a work history, leaving a job before you started it. These are important as unexplained gaps in employment history are always viewed with suspicion and so an error that might make it look like you were out of work for a year may be misinterpreted as something more sinister.

Exaggeration errors. I think it is fair to say that we've all exaggerated on a job application or CV at one time or another and it is likely an inevitable consequence of selling oneself. However, be careful how far you push the truth as the more you exaggerate something, the more likely it is going to be picked up should you make it through to interview or reference check. It is usually pretty obvious when someone is stretching the truth, especially when their claims seem to be out of proportion with their job role, for example a junior manager working for a company with a £3 million turnover saying that they single-handedly implemented an innovation that saved £1 million per year in costs.

Given the importance of avoiding errors in your applications, you need to make sure you've got a robust system in place for proofreading your work. Below are my top tips for proofreading your applications.

1. Don't start proofreading too early. Don't worry about proofreading until your application is fully written. This is a classic procrastination trick. People write the first few paragraphs of their application or covering letter, get bored or stuck, and decide to start editing and proofreading. They can spend hours trying to craft that perfect sentence, thesaurus in hand, reading, editing, re-reading, re-editing. I've seen people I know do this on multiple occasions, and I'm pretty sure I have seen this when I'm reviewing job applications. Usually what you get is a few wonderful paragraphs, written by a true wordsmith at the top of their game. However, at some point the applicant realises that the application deadline is in an hour and they've just spent the last six hours introducing themselves, explaining that they've got a first class degree and that they'd really like to come and work at my organisation. The quality of the writing that follows this realisation is somewhat less impressive than that which went before.

There is a saying that goes, "do a bad first draft, you can't edit a blank page". This is true: get as much as you can down on paper. As the entrepreneur and author Rob Moore says, "start now, get perfect later".

2. Don't rely on your computer's spellchecker.

Spellcheckers are wonderful, magical things, but they are not fool-proof. While they are getting better all the time, there are lots of errors they won't pick up, such as the incorrect use of a correctly spelled word.

3. Read it out loud. Reading your text out loud often reveals errors that you might not see on paper. A sentence that seems to make perfect sense when read in your head can sound awkward or confusing when read aloud. Reading out loud also helps you to hear your work from the perspective of the person who will be reading it.

4. Proof-listen. When you read, your brain fills in the blanks, anticipating what is coming next. This is what allows us to read so quickly. The more familiar you are with the work, the more likely your brain is to take unintended shortcuts and not actually read every word on the page. I find even when I read my own writing out loud to myself, I still miss a lot of things as I read what I think it should say, not what is actually written.

Never fear, help is at hand. For a number of years, I have been proof-listening to letters, emails, board reports and anything else I deem important enough. This has made a massive difference to my ability to spot errors in my writing. By having a neutral, computer-generated voice read your text to you, you completely eliminate reading errors. If you have written that "you graduated **form** university in 1995" your spellchecker won't necessarily pick that up, and your brain may well have assumed it said **from** as that makes logical sense, but your computer will read it to you as form not from.

You don't need any expensive equipment to do this. All modern computers have this functionality built in. If your computer is so old you don't have this functionality, or you can't get it to work, there are many free online text-to-speech tools you can use. Natural Readers (https://www.natural-readers.com/online/) is a good example. Get yourself a pair of headphones and have a play. Trust me, proof-listening will quickly become your new best friend.

5. Use friends, family and anyone else who can read. One of the most underutilised (and free) resources at your fingertips are your friends, family and colleagues. Find one or two people that you really trust and ask them to read your application and give you feedback. I suggest limiting it to one or two people as once you go above this, you start to get conflicting opinions and you end up spending more time trying to combine everyone's feedback than you do polishing your application.

People are often reticent to share their applications with others for fear of criticism or embarrassment that they might not get the job. However, you need to get over this hurdle as it creates a major block to your progress. If you don't have enough confidence in your application to share it with your mum, best friend or colleague, then you probably shouldn't be sending it anywhere else. In reality, what is there to be scared about? I've asked lots of people to read my applications over the years and not once has the person read it, thrown it back in my face and told me I've got more chance of winning Wimbledon than succeeding with that application. Most people are humbled that you've come to them for help, supportive of what you are doing, and more than happy to help. Remember, this is a two-way process: if you swallow your pride and go to someone for help, it is likely that in the future they will ask you for the same.

Be specific about what you want them to look at. It can be very frustrating if you are looking for a second pair of eyes to check the spelling and grammar, and a well-meaning friend tries to restructure your entire application for you. I break things down into spelling and grammar, structure and content.

Chapter Summary

Let's review the key points we have covered in this chapter.

- A really strong application form or CV can quickly be rejected if it contains obvious errors. Where there are lots of applicants for a job, hiring managers will actively look for reasons not to shortlist someone and basic errors provide a good justification for this.
- Spelling and grammar errors are the most common types of mistakes that get picked up on job applications, cover letters and CVs. These errors often occur because people have become too reliant on their computer's spellchecker. There are a number of tools you can use to catch these errors, such as reading your application out loud, using your computer's text-to-speech software, and getting friends and family to proofread your writing for you.
- Informational errors, such as getting the dates you started and ended jobs wrong, can also be costly. They can make it look as though you have had gaps in your employment history or that you haven't stayed in jobs for an appropriate length of time,

both of which will be viewed with suspicion by
hiring managers.

- Exaggeration errors occur when you embellish the
truth to try and make your application look more
impressive. This is something most people do to
some extent, but the bigger the exaggeration, the
greater the risk of being found out.

PART III

PREPARING FOR INTERVIEW

"Success is where preparation and opportunity meet."

- Bobby Unser

While interviews can sometimes be scary, cruel or overwhelming, the one thing they are nearly always is predictable. Before you go to the cinema, you already know that you are going to see 15 minutes of adverts, followed by a whole bunch of trailers for films you'll never watch, followed by the opening credits, then the movie and finally the closing credits. The same is almost always true of interviews. They usually start with some gentle introductions, the person leading the interview then explains the structure, if you have been asked to do a presentation that usually comes next, followed by directive questions and behavioural questions, then logistical questions, then a chance for you to ask questions, then you all shake hands again and leave. It gets even more predictable as the questions you are likely to get asked are nearly always variations on the same themes.

By understanding this process and the questions you are likely to be asked, and then preparing properly, you can take most of the mystery out of your next interview.

Prepare, prepare, prepare.

10

WHEN DOES YOUR INTERVIEW START?

sk yourself that question. When you go to a job interview, at what point in time does the interview start?

Got your answer. Good. Here's mine. It's not when the interviewer or chair of the panel has formally introduced everyone and explained the format of the interview. It's not when you get called into the interview room and nervously shake hands with the interviewer or members of the panel. It's not when you enter the building and ask for directions at the reception desk. **Your interview starts the day you find out you've got an interview.**

This seems to surprise a lot of people. Technically, you are supposed to be judged on how you perform during your formal interview as that is where you will be given scores, compared to others etc., but the reality is that every interaction you have with your potential future employers, from the moment you are selected as a candidate, should be considered part of your interview. Each one of these interactions will result in somebody forming or enhancing their opinion of you, whether positive or negative.

If you're the candidate who asks for a 10 a.m. interview slot as you've got something "really important" you need to do at 11 a.m., but then you ring the HR department to ask if you can switch to 12 noon (HR will probably ring me and ask if that's OK), only to ask to switch the time back again, what do you think that does to my impression of you? I think you're disorganised and that this job interview is not a very high priority for you right now. That's what I'll have in my mind when you walk through the door of the interview room.

When I'm interviewing, I try and get as much feedback from people as I can about a potential candidate when they're not in "interview mode". Usually a member of the HR or administration team will speak to the candidates before they go into their interview and take photocopies of their proof of ID, certificates, etc. I always try to speak to this person to get a sense of their impression of the candidates. Often people who come across as polite and friendly in an interview can show a different side when interacting with people whose opinion they don't think matters.

I once had a male candidate who came across as a nice, respectable young man during his interview. However, as I later found out, prior to interview he sat in our administration office for 15 minutes straining his neck to stare down the top of a member of the admin team to the point where she had to ask him to refrain from doing so.

I am always interested in how people interact with members of staff or other candidates before and after an interview. Often candidates will be asked to wait in an office or tea room or seating area and this is a great opportunity to see how people behave. It always pleases me when I come out of the interview room to get the next candidate and find them deep in conversation with a member of staff.

Come and Meet Me (I've already told you it's all about me)!

Throughout the recruitment process, you have the opportunity to engage with the people who are managing the hiring process. Sadly, most people are either unaware that this opportunity exists or choose not to take it. As I will explain below, taking the time to contact the hiring manager to have an informal conversation about the role can give you a number of significant advantages over the other candidates.

When applying for jobs, I will always try to have an informal conversation, ideally in person, prior to applying for the post, and if this is not possible, I will aim to do this prior to interview. If you are applying for one or two jobs, then it makes sense to do this before you apply. However, if you are someone who is on a full-blown job hunt, applying for lots of jobs, then this is probably best left until you have been offered an interview, as otherwise it will take up too much of your time.

There are many reasons why connecting with the hiring manager is so helpful. Below are five examples of why investing a small amount of your time can give you such a big advantage over other candidates.

1. **It can help you make a decision about whether you really want this job.** Jobs always look good on paper, but most people will tell you that what is

written in their job description bears little resemblance to what they actually do on a day-to-day basis. However, the things that determine if someone really enjoys their job or not tend to be the people, culture and relationships. Interviews give you a very stilted view of what it is like to work with (or for) someone as people are always on their best behaviour and are usually in sales mode. A 15-minute phone call with your future boss, cup of coffee with potential co-workers or tour of the department will give you a much better sense of if this is actually somewhere you can see yourself fitting in.

2. **It can give you inside information you can use during the interview.** An informal phone call or meeting, prior to either you submitting an application or you attending an interview, is like a free gift of information. You can ask questions about the role, the department, future plans, threats and opportunities to the organisation, culture and pretty much anything you think is relevant. When it comes to writing an application or attending an interview, you will be so much better informed than the other candidates who have not taken this opportunity that it is almost unfair.

3. **It removes the initial fear barrier.** Have you ever been on a blind date? Most people find that first date scary. You have so many questions about the other person and no answers. What if you don't like them? What if they don't like you? What do they look like? Are they polite or rude? However, if you get as far as a second date, all that anxiety and anticipation is gone. You have a good sense of the

person and you have made the decision that they are someone you might be able to form a relationship with. Job interviews are no different. It is a very different sensation walking into an interview with a person or panel of people you've never met before versus walking into an interview where you have a level of familiarity with at least one other person in the room, who is likely to be the person responsible for hiring you.

4. **You can create a personal connection.** In the course of speaking to or meeting with your future boss, you are both likely to share some personal information about yourselves. I believe that given enough time, most people can find some sort of common connections around their lives. These often relate to where people grew up or went to university, people they know, interests in sports, music, travel and a whole list of other things. Forming a personal connection elevates you from being just another faceless name on an interview schedule to a person with whom the interviewer shares something. This can be very powerful.

5. **You will immediately score points for effort.** The very act of making contact and asking for the opportunity to speak or meet with the person responsible for the recruitment, or a member of the team, will score you major brownie points. Not only does it reflect your effort, but it also shows that you are serious about this job.

Chapter Summary

Let's review the key points we have covered in this chapter.

- Your interview starts the moment you find out you've been invited to an interview. Every interaction you have with the organisation considering hiring you from that point may well influence the hiring manager's impression of you.
- Speaking to or meeting with the hiring manager (or a member of their team) is a great way to get yourself ahead of other candidates.
- Having a conversation with the person responsible for recruiting gives you an opportunity to form a relationship with this person and gain some inside information about the job. At the application stage, you are simply a name on a sheet of paper, but a meeting or phone call makes it far more likely that the recruiting manager will remember you (and hopefully have a positive opinion of you) when you come to interview.
- Most employers view someone making the effort to speak to them prior to interview as a sign of professionalism and commitment. This can only improve your chances of success.

11

THINGS YOU SHOULD KNOW BEFORE INTERVIEW

I t amazes me how many people get to the stage of interview knowing next to nothing about the organisation they are hoping to work for, or the industry they are trying to move into. These days, 30 minutes spent on the internet can give you a pretty thorough overview of most organisations. Here are a few key bits of information I would expect any applicant who stands a chance of me hiring them to know.

1. What are the company's mission, vision and values? These days nearly all organisations have these, and usually share them openly on their websites, recruiting materials, etc. Don't just read and memorise them, but spend some time thinking about what they mean and how you could help the company to achieve them.

2. What does the company do? What is the main purpose of the company? What is their industry and sector? The way I like to frame this (and the way I often ask candidates about this in an interview) is, if you met up with some friends tonight and told them you'd just been offered a job at The

Big Widget Company, how would you describe to your friends what The Big Widget Company does?

3. What does the specific department that you would be working in do? Similar to question 2, what is the main purpose of your future department? How would you describe the critical role your department plays in the company to your grandparents or other relatives?

4. What recent news and events have occurred? What has happened to the organisation recently that you should know about? Have they opened a new store, hired a new CEO, lost a major contract or just won an award for being a fantastic employer?

5. What is it like to work for the organisation? There are lots of ways to find out about life inside a company. You can look online and see how people rate the employer. Companies like glassdoor.com give star ratings (provided by users) for companies as well as a "would you recommend this company to a friend" score. You can also look at the information the organisation provides, but as you would expect, this is usually a very biased source of information.

By far the best way to get a sense of what it is really like to work for a company is to talk to people who already work there. In today's interconnected world, it is pretty easy to find someone who knows someone who works at the organisation you are considering. Sites like Facebook and LinkedIn make a search like this very easy. Aside from being a great way for you to find out about the organisation, you will score lots of brownie points in an interview if you slip in that you've taken the time to speak to a few people who work at the company.

As I mentioned earlier, I love it when people make the effort to come and see me prior to an interview. If you do choose to do this (and I highly recommend it), ask if you can speak to some of the employees and find out a bit more about the organisation and the people you will be working with.

6. Who will be interviewing you? Knowing a bit about the person or people who are going to be interviewing you can be extremely helpful, especially for more senior positions. There are a number of reasons for this. Firstly, it gives you a sense of familiarity. If you haven't been able to meet the hiring manager before the interview, then the first time you meet them is when you walk through that door. However, if you've spent some time trying to find out a bit about this person, maybe you've seen their picture online, and know a bit about their history, when you finally meet them it gives you a sense that you know them already.

Secondly, by knowing something about the people interviewing you, it gives you a chance to find personal connections. Reading someone's biography on a website or LinkedIn profile can tell you a lot about a person's life, such as where they went to school (and therefore where they grew up), if they went to university (and if so where and what did they study), where they have worked, what their interests are, do they have children, etc. I believe that most people share at least one common interest with every other person, you just have to take the time to look for it. These connections can be very powerful. If you spot that both you and your interviewer went to the University of Middle Earth, when you're talking about your education, don't just say, "I got my undergraduate degree from the University of Middle Earth"; instead, add in that it was a great place to study or it was located in a fantastic town. This offers the interviewer (who, having read your application or CV, is already aware of the connection) the opportunity to mention that they too went to Middle Earth, at which point they might ask you where you lived or if a certain pub was still there. A connection is born.

When you get invited to interview you usually get told who will be on the panel. If you don't, it is perfectly reasonable to ask. I usually create a grid with the names of the people interviewing me down the left-hand column. I then add their job title in the next box, add in a picture of them if I can find one, and then any other information I can find on them in the final box. By doing this, by the time I walk through the door and shake their hands, I feel like I know them. This also makes it much easier to remember people's names during the interview (an example form is included at www.howtogethired.co.uk).

7. **What is your elevator pitch?** You may have heard the term elevator pitch used in the context of people who are trying to start a new business or venture. The idea is that if you suddenly found yourself in a lift with your ideal investor or business partner, and you only had 60 seconds before the person reached their floor and departed, could you pitch your business idea to them, covering all the key bits of information, in that time. It isn't about speaking really quickly and trying to cram a 10-minute presentation into 60 seconds, it's about distilling all of the most important information and delivering it in a calm, logical way.

During my MBA we were taught to develop a "personal elevator pitch". Instead of selling a business idea or investment opportunity, the asset we were selling was ourselves. Initially we wrote down personal biographies, covering all of the information we thought a prospective recruiter would want to know about us, starting with education, moving through experience, skills and knowledge, touching on us as individuals and then ending with our ambitions. As you can imagine, for some people this biography ran across multiple pages. The next step was to turn the biography into a spoken sales pitch. Again, these could be quite lengthy. Then we would practise them over and over in front of the mirror, until our pitches were concise and had a conversational rhythm to them. The final step was to test them. This was done in a giant lecture theatre with about a hundred other MBA students. The best way to describe it is probably speed dating. You would find someone you didn't know, introduce yourself, give your 60-second pitch, and the other person would give you feedback on how you could improve it. Then it would be their turn to pitch to you. We did this over and over again, each time honing our pitches based on the feedback we received. By the end of the day, I think I had probably pitched to 50 people and could deliver my pitch in my sleep.

I would recommend that anyone who is in the process of looking for a job develop their own personal elevator pitch. I realise that not everyone has the luxury of a room full of willing participants to provide feedback on your pitch, but we all have friends and family, most of whom would spare a few minutes to listen to you and give you some pointers. The confidence that having a pre-prepared pitch, which you can adapt to any given situation, gives you is invaluable.

Internal Candidates

Many of the things we have talked about in the preceding pages make the assumption that you are applying for a job at an organisation that you do not currently work at, and for the majority of people this will be the case. If this applies to you, then please feel free to skip to the next chapter. For those who are considering a move internally within their organisation, please read on.

Hiring an internal candidate is often more complicated than hiring an outsider. This is because people make a number of assumptions and misjudgements about how the process differs for them as a result of being internal. It is easy to assume that the people on the interview panel know you, like you, and are familiar with your work, and therefore the interview is more of a box-ticking exercise than a "real interview". Unfortunately, these assumptions often lead to people performing poorly at interview, often resulting in them not getting the job. Below are some important points to consider as an internal candidate.

1. **When applying for a job you will be judged on your application, interview and references.** This is a really important point to understand. Candidates often assume that the panel's prior knowledge of them is what they will be making their decision on, and thus don't put the effort into the recruitment process that external candidates do. While it is impossible to prevent your experience of someone from influencing your thinking, panel members have to make decisions based on the evidence presented to them during the recruitment process so that there is an even playing field for both external and internal candidates. Therefore, I would suggest preparing for an interview as if you were an

external candidate, with the interviewers knowing nothing about you other than what you have told them in your application.

2. Don't exaggerate. It is common knowledge that everyone stretches the truth a little bit during job interviews. People's previous experiences become broader, responsibilities become wider, budgets become bigger and results become more impressive. For external candidates, it is easy to exaggerate a bit: as long as you don't go overboard, it is unlikely you will ever get found out. However, for internal candidates, this is a much riskier game. An exaggeration from an external candidate becomes a flat-out lie from an internal candidate, no matter how small. The price for being caught in a lie is much higher than the benefit you are likely to gain.

3. Show enthusiasm. Another assumption internal candidates tend to make is that the panel already know that the applicant really wants the job. When an external candidate interviews for a job, they usually know very little about what the job will actually be like, and they focus their attention on the positive things they have seen in the job description and personal specification. Internal candidates tend to have a much better comprehension of the job, understanding both the positives and the negatives. As a result, internal candidates often seem flat in interviews when compared to the enthusiastic newcomer. It is important that you make a conscious effort to show the panel how enthusiastic you are about the role.

4. Understand your reputation. As an internal candidate, one big advantage you do have is access to the people that will be interviewing you. During the recruitment process, you should take any opportunity you can to speak directly to these people about the role, their expectations and, if possible, what their thoughts on you are. It is often easiest done before you have actually applied for the job when you can ask to meet with someone and tell them that you are "considering" applying for the job and ask for their thoughts. At this stage in the process, they are far more likely to be open with you. This will help you to understand what your reputation within the organisation is and if there are specific areas of perceived weakness you need to address during the interview.

5. Sell yourself and back up your claims with examples. Sometimes in interviews internal candidates don't get (or take) the same opportunity to sell themselves as other candidates. If one of the standard questions is "give us an example of when you have been involved in implementing a new IT system" and everyone knows that last year the interviewee helped to install an important new payroll system, a candidate might be tempted to give a very short answer along the lines of "as I'm sure you're all aware, last year I led the implementation team for the new payroll system, which all went really well". Both the candidate and the panel make the assumption that they can fill in the blanks, and everyone moves on to the next question. However, this robs the candidate of the opportunity to make sure everyone understands what a challenge this was and how well they performed during the implementation. It is risky to assume that this is what all of the panel members are thinking, when in fact their memory of the implementation might be that on two occasions staff got paid late and they had to deal with the fallout.

6. Remind the panel of the advantages of an internal

candidate. There are a number of very obvious advantages to hiring internally. Because the advantages are obvious, candidates often make the assumption that an interview panel will have already considered them, but it never hurts to make sure the panel are reminded of them. In your responses, look for opportunities to highlight advantages, for instance the fact that as you are internal, your notice period might be a lot shorter, and once you're in post, you wouldn't take three to six months to settle into the organisation like other candidates might. Also try to remind the panel of the risks of hiring an unknown quantity rather than someone who is known and trusted within the organisation. This is also a chance to highlight your loyalty to the company; you're someone who sees themselves working there for the long term, not someone who hops from job to job.

Much as it might seem painful at times, the best tactic is to simply play the role of an external candidate to avoid making any risky assumptions. Make sure your application, CV, cover letter and interview performance are all good enough to get you to the next stage on their own merit, and don't rely on people being aware of your reputation.

Chapter Summary

Let's review the key points we have covered in this chapter.

- There is some basic, but very important, information about the organisation you are interviewing with that you should always know before stepping into the interview room. This includes high-level information about what the organisation does, what its values are, and specific information about the area of the organisation you will be working in. Most of this information is freely available on the internet and shouldn't take more than 30 minutes to find.

- You should also find out as much as you can about the people interviewing you. This will help you to feel a level of familiarity with the panel and may allow you to find a common connection with some of the panel members.
- Having a personal elevator pitch that you have written down, rehearsed and memorised will allow you to answer questions about yourself with confidence and clarity.
- Being an internal candidate has a number of advantages and disadvantages. The best strategy is to prepare for an interview as if you were an external candidate and not make any assumptions about what the panel members know about you and your work.

12

THE MOST COMMON INTERVIEW QUESTIONS AND HOW TO ANSWER THEM

I searched a range of publications and websites, both UK based and international, that list the "most commonly asked interview questions". As you would imagine, most come up with very similar questions and themes, usually worded in slightly different ways. Using these different sources, I have created the list of nine questions below. Please note that I haven't included any behavioural questions (e.g. give us an example of a time when you have...) as I will cover these separately in the next chapter.

1. What can you tell me about yourself?
2. What are your strengths?
3. What weaknesses do you have?
4. Why should I consider hiring you?
5. Where do you see yourself five years from now?
6. Why do you want this job/Why do you want to work here?
7. What motivates you?
8. Is there anything you would like to ask me?
9. What is your salary expectation?

Let's take them one by one.

Question 1: What can you tell me about yourself?

This is your classic "break the candidates in gently" question. It is usually the first question asked and it seems like an easy opening as there are no right or wrong answers, but beware. Early impressions are so important and while technically there might not be right or wrong answers, there are certainly answers that can bore the pants off any interviewer or reveal too much information to the panel (you'd be surprised what people volunteer under the pressure of interview when asked an open question like this).

This question may read "What can you tell me about yourself?" but you should not see this as an open invitation to take the interview panel on a meandering journey of your life, with no limitation on subject matter or time. When you hear this question, please translate it into something along the lines of "please take a couple of minutes to talk us through your education, career and personal endeavours to date, focusing on the things that you think are most relevant to preparing you for this role". Bear in mind that the panel will have already seen your application, cover letter or CV, so don't just regurgitate what you've already told them. Use this as an opportunity to sell your achievements and give them an insight into you as an individual at the same time. The vast majority of your interview will be focused on your qualifications, skills and experience, and so this first question may be the only opportunity you get to show who you are as a person, and why you are so awesome. Don't miss this opportunity.

As this is the most commonly asked question, you can be

pretty sure that you are going to be asked it (or some variation on it). Therefore, there should be no excuse for not
having a well-crafted and rehearsed response ready to go.
This is where your personal elevator pitch we talked about
in the last chapter comes in. If you've worked out your pitch
and taken the time to practise it until it is ingrained in your
memory, then this question becomes a question you should
look forward to being asked. As it is often the first question
asked, nailing this one will not only give you great confidence, but will also help to capture the interview panel's
interest in you.

**Questions 2 and 3: What are your strengths? What
weaknesses do you have?**

We'll take these two together as they are often asked as a
pair, and the logic in answering them applies equally to
strengths and weaknesses. This question is a great test of
two very important things: i) how prepared you are and ii)
whether you can smell your own BS.

Preparation. When you get asked about your strengths and
weaknesses, the panel rarely cares about your answers. As it
is such a commonly asked question, it is used to gauge how
much preparation you have done for the interview. If you
can answer this simple question without thinking, it is a
sign that you've taken at least a bit of time to research the
most commonly asked questions and come up with an
answer. If you look blank and say something along the lines
of "hmmm, that's an interesting question, well I guess I'm,
um, people say that when they err need help, you know if
they're really busy or something, then I will, you know, help
them, even if I'm really busy myself. So, I guess selfless. Is

that a strength?", then you're probably going to be in for a rough ride.

Smelling your own BS. This is one question where people tend to take more than a little liberty with the truth. I'm all for selling yourself, but people often lose perspective of what sounds reasonable. Here are a few examples of some weaknesses I've heard over the years.

"I think my biggest weakness is that people are often intimidated by me as I tend to be better at most things than them."
"My biggest weakness is probably that I just care too much."
"My biggest weakness is that I'm a perfectionist."
"My biggest weakness is probably my efficiency. In my last job my line manager found it hard to find tasks or projects for me as I got them done so quickly."
"Without doubt my biggest weakness is I'm a workaholic."

And my all-time favourite:

"I've thought about this a lot as I knew you'd ask this question and, honestly, I don't think I have any weaknesses."

Now I hope as you read through the examples above you realise how ridiculous they sound, and so you should. The test here is simple. Assuming you have thought about this question in advance and prepared your answer, how good is your internal filter? If you've given it some thought and you've come to the conclusion that saying you simply have no weaknesses, or that you struggle with being so much more intelligent than everyone else around you, is a sensible answer that reflects well on you, then you are not the sort of person I want as part of my team.

Tips on answering

Naming your strengths and weaknesses shouldn't be that hard. We all have them. My advice is be honest. Ask your friends, family and colleagues and see what they think. When you offer your weaknesses, present a mitigating action. For instance, if you say one of your weaknesses is public speaking, then add in that you have signed up for a public speaking course to help you develop this (don't lie – you actually have to do it if you're going to say it).

It is important to be able to back up whatever you say with examples. For instance, if you say one of your strengths is that you are always willing to go above and beyond what is expected of you in your job role, make sure you have a good example of when you have actually done that. It is very embarrassing when someone makes a claim about themselves, and then when asked for an examples says "I can't think of any, but it is definitely true".

Question 4: Why should I consider hiring you?

If question 1 (What can you tell me about yourself?) was a broad opportunity to tell the panel who you are, touching on why you'd be perfect for the job, then this question is where you go to town. If, when preparing your application, you took the time to go through the personal specification and matched your qualifications, skills and experience to the job requirements (see Chapter 5), then you've already done all the hard work. From the job advert, job description, personal specification and any conversations you've had with your interviewers, you should have a pretty good idea of what the panel are looking for. This question is simply demonstrating how you tick all these boxes.

Many people answer this question by simply listing as many attributes about themselves (perceived or real) as they can. It can turn into a very long list, for example "well I'm very organised, kind, am very detail focused, happy to work long hours, am a real team player.". This is just listing positive attributes, which anyone can do, but lacks any real substance.

The trick to answering this question successfully is making sure you do two things. Firstly, match the attributes you give with the ones they are looking for. If I am hiring someone to work as part of a close-knit team, telling me how well you work on your own isn't likely to impress me a great deal.

Secondly, qualify what you say rather than just providing a long list. If one of the criteria of the job is presenting to the board from time to time, saying "one of the reasons you should hire me is I'm comfortable presenting to the board" is somewhat helpful. However, if you qualify that by saying "one of the reasons you should hire me is I'm comfortable presenting to the board, as I have done this on a regular basis in my current role", I'm more likely to believe you. I might then ask a follow-up question to see if you were telling the truth (e.g. what was the subject of your presentation the most recent time you presented to the board?). As long as you're telling the truth, you then have a further opportunity to impress me.

Question 5: Where do you see yourself five years from now?

I find this a very hard question to answer, and not all that useful when interviewing others. Despite this, many people like asking this question (or variations such as two, three, ten or twenty years) so let's have a look at answering it.

When you answer this question, you walk a tightrope between two very bad responses. At one end there is the uninspiring, unambitious option. This is where the candidate's answer indicates that they hope to be in the same job from tomorrow until the day they retire. They show no inclination that they want to develop or get promoted in time. These individuals are usually a nightmare to manage, and often from the day you hire them you have to start working out how to get rid of them.

At the other end of the tightrope are the super-ambitious people, who know exactly where they want to be in five years, and it isn't still working for you. In reality, there is nothing wrong with this – in fact I applaud it – but you have to be very careful in the way you phrase it. Often people's answers give the impression that as soon as they have learned what they can from the job, they'll be off to bigger and better places. Again, nothing wrong with wanting to progress your career, but this kind of attitude often frightens recruiters away. Employing and developing someone is a big investment, not just financially, but also in terms of time and emotional energy. If I think that you're going to jump ship as soon as possible, I am less likely to make that investment.

A good answer I heard recently was as follows: "Right now I'm looking to join an organisation where I can learn and grow. I hope once I've found my feet and fully understand the role there will be opportunities for me to develop and take on more responsibilities. For example, I've always enjoyed people management in the past so that might be an area I can develop. I'm not sure exactly what I'll be doing in five years' time, but hopefully still working here at Pink Panther Publishing in a more senior role."

I like this answer as it seems humble and honest. It gives the impression that the individual is keen to develop their skills, but isn't going to run off to another company for more money the minute they finish their training.

Question 6: Why do you want this job/Why do you want to work here?

Like the others in this list, this is a question that you need to have an answer ready for. The question can be interpreted more broadly to say the following:

1. What do you know about this firm/company/department?
2. Given what you know, why do you want to work here?

When a lot of people get asked why they want to work for their new potential employer, they often answer a different question: "Why do you want to leave your current job?" This is a very different question which has a very different answer. People will tell you what's wrong with their current employer, or why they are ready for a change, or why this job would be a perfect fit for them. As I have now mentioned many times, this is all about me and making me feel special. Therefore, telling me why your current employer is rubbish or that you really want to work as a marketing manager will do little for me. I want you to show me that you have actually done some research about my organisation, you understand what we do, what our values are, and why it is an awesome organisation to work for. I then want you to tell me why who we are fits with who you are, and why we could be great together.

If you've done the preparation described at the beginning of the last chapter, then you should have no problem answering this question. Again, this is a great opportunity to impress, and all you need to do is spend 30 minutes researching the company. A small price to pay if it is the difference between being offered a job or continuing your job search!

Question 7: What motivates you?

This question is often difficult to answer, but is critically important. If I'm going to be managing someone, it is really important for me to understand what gets them fired up to come to work every day and give 100%. For example, you might be someone who requires high-level positive feedback from your boss. On the one hand, as a manager this can be very tiring and time-consuming, but on the other hand, if all it takes is a pat on the back and some genuine praise to get you motivated, it is a motivator that I am in control of. However, if your motivation is driven by money, it will require little of my time and effort during the year, but will require me to continually increase your compensation year on year for fear you will leave the company or become unmotivated.

In Chapter 1, we explored how to better understand what motivates you. If you didn't do this earlier, I strongly recommend going back and working through the exercise. People often get stuck on this question as they genuinely don't know the answer. Taking 30 minutes of your time to understand yourself better will pay for itself many times over.

From the research you have done about the company (see Chapter 11), you should by now have a good sense of what the company's mission, vision and values are. The interviewers will likely be looking to see if what motivates you is in line with the values of the company. Usually by the very nature of the fact that you've applied for a given job, it is likely that there will be some alignment between the two. If you are applying for a job at a non-profit organisation, it is unlikely that your major motivation will be making money.

Below are some examples of good answers I have heard recently. However, they are only good answers if you genuinely mean them and they fit with the job you are interviewing for:

- I am a very goal-oriented person. I enjoy setting a goal, working out the steps I need to take to achieve it, and then reaching the goal.
- I love learning. As long as I am learning new things, I tend to stay interested. (This can be professional or personal.)
- I enjoy knowing that what I am doing is having a positive impact on people's lives. I don't like sitting in an office all day, treating people as lines on a spreadsheet. I like the look in people's eyes when something I've been involved in has made their life better.
- I am motivated by developing my staff. I like taking on new hires that don't know a thing about our business and developing them into confident and

competent individuals who are an asset to our team.

Question 8: Is there anything that you would like to ask me?

This is your chance to leave a good impression. On a busy day of interviewing, when I've asked ten candidates the same questions, most of which have very similar answers, remembering each candidate's response can be very difficult. However, it is much easier for me to remember the questions interviewees ask me, as they tend to be far more varied and therefore easier to associate with an individual. This means that your questions to the interview panel can often have as much impact on the panel's impression of you as all their questions to you.

What if I don't have any questions?

Not asking any questions is usually not a good idea. There are, however, a number of circumstances where it is OK:

- If you have met the hiring manager before your interview and so have had ample opportunity to ask all your questions.
- If there has been a less formal part of the interview, for instance taking a tour of the building, where you have had the opportunity to ask lots of questions.
- When it has been a very conversational interview and you've had the opportunity to ask lots of questions along the way.

In any of these circumstances (or similar situations when

you have had a genuine chance to ask questions prior to the interview), make sure you share this with the panel, as they may not know that you've already taken an opportunity to ask questions. For example, when asked the question don't simply say no, but say that when you met with Mr Smith informally last week, you had the opportunity to ask him most of your questions, and the rest have been covered during the interview.

Things you should not ask

Asking ill-advised questions at the end of an interview can be worse than not asking any at all. Sometimes candidates who have had a fantastic interview can undo a lot of their hard work with a few misplaced questions. There are three key types of questions you should avoid:

1. Specific things about the benefits you would get, for example salary, how much leave you get (asking about leave or sickness benefit gives the impression that you're already thinking about not being at work), or whether you get your own office, are all things that you can ask when they ring up and offer you the job.

2. Questions that you should already know or could have already found out. Asking these sorts of questions (e.g. what are the values of the organisation? or what exactly does this department do?) gives the impression that you couldn't be bothered to do any research in preparation for the interview. Even worse than this is when someone asks a question that is answered in the job description you've provided them, for example what will my main

responsibilities be or will I have to manage other people?

3. Yes or no questions. This is your opportunity to engage with the panel and get them to open up to you. Asking closed questions wastes this opportunity and makes it look like you are just asking questions for the sake of asking questions.

Good questions to ask

It is very hard to suggest suitable questions as they vary so much depending on the specific role and organisation you are interviewing with. However, below are some of my favourite questions that I have either been asked during an interview or asked myself.

- If I was successful in getting the job, and in a year's time we were sitting down for my annual appraisal, what would you have expected me to have achieved in that time?
- What are the biggest challenges facing the company/department/team right now?
- What do you like best about working here?
- Can you describe what a typical day in this role might look like?
- What development opportunities might be available to me in the future?
- How would you describe the culture here?
- What is the background to the role? Is it a new position or is someone being replaced? (If someone is being replaced, you could ask why they left.)
- If I am successful, what would my induction period be like?

Question 9: What is your salary expectation?

This is a question commonly asked during an interview in many parts of the world. It is unlikely you will be asked this if you are interviewing for a public sector post in the UK; however, it may come up if you're being interviewed in a commercial setting. If it doesn't come up in the interview, it will inevitably come up at some point for the successful candidate (i.e. you) so you may as well spend some time thinking about how you would answer this question.

When I am the candidate being interviewed, I always hope this question doesn't come up. The reason for this is that by showing your hand, you pass the power to the hiring manager. I like to get through the interview process, for the panel to sit down and discuss all the candidates, and for them to decide that I'm the one they want, without considering the cost. It is very rare for an interview panel to change its mind once it has chosen their preferred candidate, so I know that if I get the call offering me the job, they are far more likely to meet my salary requirements than to retract their offer and go to their second choice. However, if they ask about salary during the interview, and my answer is somewhat higher than other candidates' expectations, it may influence their decision to offer me the post.

In Chapter 1, we talked about identifying your requirements for your new job, including the level of compensation you are looking for. As you move through the recruitment process, you may find that you move the goalposts depending on how much you want to work for an organisation. For instance, if you've found your dream job, you may be willing to work for less money than you originally thought. However, the process you went through in Chapter

1 should give you a good idea of what your realistic, but positive, salary is.

If you are asked about your salary expectations in an interview, as with most situations discussed in this book, my advice is to be honest. Don't undersell yourself, but don't come out with something so outrageous that you price yourself out of consideration. Answers that usually go down well are more related to your payment over the long term. Take these two different answers to the question:

- **Candidate 1**: My expectation would be at least £40,000 per year.
- **Candidate 2**: If I had to give you a number I would like around £40,000 a year. However, I would be willing to work for a smaller base salary if there were opportunities to grow my income, either through performance-related pay or promotions over the long term.

In this scenario, Candidate 2 is backing themselves to thrive in the job. This gives the panel confidence that this person believes they can add real value to the team.

How to prepare your answers

Once you've had a think about the answers to these questions, it is time to properly prepare your answers. I do this using a question matrix. This is a simple grid that has all the questions you think you're likely to be asked in the first column and your answers in the second column. I would start with the nine questions listed above and then add your own questions to the list based on your knowledge of the company, the individuals interviewing you, the job description, and the personal specification. A copy of the question matrix is available at www.howtogethired.co.uk.

Going through the process of writing down your answers, then reading them, editing them and repeating the cycle has two massive benefits. Firstly, it means that your answers will be far better crafted than if you were to come up with the answer on the fly during the interview. Secondly, it will give you confidence going into the interview that if you get asked any of those questions, you have a polished, rehearsed response memorised.

Chapter Summary

Let's review the key points we have covered in this chapter.

- There are a small number of interview questions that appear regularly in job interviews. While the exact way these questions are asked will differ from interview to interview, the basic premise of the questions remains constant. Having pre-prepared answers to these questions that you can adapt to the context of the question can remove a significant amount of the pressure people feel in interviews.
- The nine most common interview questions are:

  1. What can you tell me about yourself?
  2. What are your strengths?
  3. What weaknesses do you have?
  4. Why should I consider hiring you?
  5. Where do you see yourself five years from now?
  6. Why do you want this job/Why do you want to work here?

7. What motivates you?

8. Is there anything that you would like to ask me?

9. What is your salary expectation?

- Behind each of these questions is a logical reason as to why recruiters ask them. For many of the questions, there is a subtext that may not initially be obvious. By understanding what the person interviewing you wants to learn from your answer, you can ensure that your response is appropriate.

- Using an answer sheet or matrix grid to write down your answers will help you to both prepare great answers and also memorise them ahead of your interview.

13

GIVE US AN EXAMPLE OF A TIME WHEN... (BEHAVIOURAL QUESTIONS)

Now you've listed the questions you think you might get asked in your question matrix, it is time to consider how you prepare your answers for one of the most common types of question, often called behavioural questions. Think of these as any question that starts with "Please tell us about a time when you have..." Below are some common examples of these types of questions.

- Please tell us about a time when you have shown leadership in a difficult situation.
- Please tell us about a time when you have had to use your initiative to solve a problem.
- Please tell us about a time when you have had to deal with conflict in the workplace.
- Please tell us about a time when you have delivered change to a system or organisation.
- Please tell us about a time when you have been asked to improve performance.

- Please tell us about a time when you have had to make a difficult decision.
- Please tell us about a time when you have gone above and beyond to help someone/to deliver a target for your organisation.

They may be framed in a slightly different way (e.g. "Tell me about a situation in the past...") but the basic principle is exactly the same. I both love and hate these types of questions in equal measure. I love them as they give a fantastic insight into an individual and tell the interviewers far more about someone than very closed questions. They represent a great opportunity for a candidate to take the floor and wow the panel with their experience. Conversely, I hate these questions because people generally answer them so badly.

There are three very simple things I want to know when I ask a question like this.

1. What was the problem / task / issue / scenario you faced?
2. What did **you** do?
3. What was the outcome?

Most people tick all these boxes when giving their answer, but they present them in a confusing order, surround them in irrelevant detail and lose sight of their personal role in the example they are giving. As I mentioned several times in the application section, a big part of your job is to make my life as easy as possible. Therefore, if I have to sit and listen to a long rambling answer where I have to try and pick out the key points of your story, then you're making me work too hard. On the other hand, if you put it on a plate for me with a well-structured, concise answer, then I'm far more likely to remember all the wonderful things you've just told me about yourself.

At this point I want to introduce the SAR structure for framing answers to these types of questions. SAR stands for Situation, Action, Result and is a commonly used technique I have found very useful over the years. Let's look at each of the three elements in more detail.

Situation – A brief background of the scenario that you were facing. What was the problem? Why was it a problem? Who was involved? What were you trying to achieve?

People often fail to make clear what the specific problem they are trying to address is. To the narrator this is always blindingly obvious, but when someone launches into a complex story it can often be challenging for the interviewers to pick out the specifics of the challenge being described.

Action – What action did you take? All too often people start by talking about themselves but quickly move to using terms like "we" or "the team" when describing what actions were taken. This always weakens their answer as it is never clear whether what happened was actually a result of their personal efforts, or whether they were merely part of a team that delivered the positive outcome. This is a chance for you to showcase your fantastic work, so make sure that you're the hero of your own story.

Result – What actually happened in the end? Everything that is said before is pointless if you don't share the positive results of what you achieve. The more specific you can be the better, and if you can include numbers that's fantastic. I am far more likely to remember your answer if you tell me you "reduced the cost of something by 30%" rather than saying that you "saved a lot of money for the company". Similarly, saying that you "doubled productivity" is a lot more memorable than saying "we were able to make a lot more widgets".

It is worth noting here that many people use the STAR structure as opposed to SAR, with the T standing for Task. In my mind, explaining what the task is becomes hard to separate from explaining what the situation is, so I prefer to fold the two in together. I also think people like STAR as the acronym as it is slightly catchier than SAR. Whether you want to use SAR, STAR or any other system, it doesn't matter; the key is using something to help you structure your responses to these sorts of questions.

Preparing to answer behavioural questions by writing down your answers in the SAR format and practising delivering them gives you the best chance of being able to showcase the great work you have done. If you don't prepare these questions in advance, you put a huge amount of pressure on yourself to not only think of a suitable example on the spot, but also structure it in a way that is coherent. To illustrate the points above, let's work through an example of a common behavioural question.

Please give us an example of when you have used your own initiative to solve a problem.

Below is the sort of example I would expect from someone who has to a) think of an example off the top of their head and b) try and formulate that example into a response that fits the question being asked.

Version 1

I was working for this company that made floral displays; it was just a summer job that I did for about three months. We made displays which people ordered either online or by phone. After a few weeks I started trying to guess what people were going to order that day as we spent a lot of time sitting around or working manically depending on the orders. There were about ten of us working at any one time. It wasn't great as we'd miss a lot of delivery deadlines. Some of the bouquets were really complicated – there was one called the Blueberry Bloom that had chrysanthemum and blueberry roses which was so complicated it took twice as long as most of the other bouquets. I told my manager that I thought some displays were ordered more than others at certain times. So, we changed the system to make some displays in advance which we thought might be used during the day. It worked pretty well. Before we changed the system, we did a pilot to test this. It wasn't just based on what I'd found; we also looked at the order database for the last six months. As I said, it worked pretty well. It meant that we were busy all day rather than just at certain times, as the number of orders went up after we'd done it. The number of times that the express deliveries were used also went down, which was really good as they were a lot more expensive.

Now let's revisit the same example, but this time given by someone who identified this example as one they could possibly use in an interview and who had prepared the story using the SAR structure. I've used the same information as in the response above, but I've added in some specific details.

Version 2

> **Situation:** I was working for an organisation that produced floral displays that were ordered by phone or online. Due to the perishable nature of the flowers and large number of different products available for order, the displays were made in real time; in other words, as soon as an order was confirmed, we would make it. This meant that the work demand would be very variable, so staff would spend a lot of time sitting around waiting for orders to come in and then suddenly we would have manic periods trying to get multiple orders filled before the delivery deadline of our courier, which we often missed and then had to pay extra for an express delivery. There were usually about ten people on a shift, which was about the right number of people needed to meet the peaks in demand, but at other times seemed very excessive for the low volume of work.

> **Action:** After working there for a few weeks, I started to get a feel for what the customers usually ordered and when, and so I started to make predictions each morning of the types of orders we would receive. Once I had done this for a few weeks and felt confident there were some patterns that could be

predicted, I met with my line manager and shared my findings. Together we went through six months of previous orders to back up the data I had collected myself. We identified four different products that were the most commonly ordered displays at specific times. Based on this data I was asked to conduct a pilot, making ten of each of the four displays during the quiet times in anticipation of them being ordered that day.

Result: The pilot proved to be very successful and so we extended the scope to make the nine most common displays in advance. We found that the cost benefit of making these displays in advance far outweighed the lost revenue of any displays that were made and not sold. We even started discounting any pre-made displays we thought we might not sell on the website to avoid leftover stock. As a result we managed to increase our production capacity by over 20% and reduce our use of the expensive express deliveries by over 60%.

Let's have a look at some of the differences between the two versions. The first version gets across all of the key points that the candidate wants to get across, but they don't all fall into a logical order. That's just how our brains work when we're thinking of things on the fly. As you talk, you think of details that are important to the story but you don't have time to stop and organise your thoughts, so you tend to say them as you think of them. The second version is easier to follow as the answer is structured. The information is provided in a logical order that makes it very easy for the audience to follow.

You will also notice that there are some odd details in the first version that don't really add anything to the narrative and seem a bit out of place. Specifically, the sentences about the job being a summer job that they only did for three months and the complex "Blueberry Bloom" display. These are what I call "thinking time" phrases. They occur when people launch into their answer without really knowing what they are going to say and suddenly need a few seconds to think about what they are going to say next. Rather than pause and take a few seconds to think and compose their thoughts, as most people would do in normal conversation, they instead fill the void with meaningless details that fly into their heads. There are a number of disadvantages to doing this. Firstly, people often end up sounding incoherent as they jump from one thing to another. Secondly, it is a lot harder to think clearly about how you are going to structure the next part of your answer while talking at the same time. Try it. Finally, it can lead to one of the worst interview crimes: the tangent trap (more on this shortly).

As I mentioned earlier, how much involvement the candidate has actually had in delivering the outcomes they are describing is often not clear. In the first version, it is clear that the candidate is responsible for the original idea (that some displays could be made in advance), but once they make their manager aware of the idea, it is hard to tell how involved the candidate is in actually implementing the change. Compare this with the second version, where the candidate says that together with their line manager they looked at six months of previous data and that they were asked to conduct a pilot. In the second version, the story-teller is definitely the hero!

Finally, look at how the outcome is described in the two

versions. They are essentially describing the same two points: firstly, the increase in orders due to more efficient use of staff members' time, and secondly, a reduction in the use of express deliveries which results in a cost saving. However, version two gives us a much better sense of the scale of success. In the first version the candidate says "it worked pretty well". As an interviewer, this would not impress me. I would be left wondering just how successful the bright idea of theirs had actually been, and would probably ask a pointed follow-up question in order to find the answer. I would also be disappointed by the candidate's lack of attention to detail in not even having a vague idea as to the scale of the improvement.

When preparing for an interview, I create a grid with the questions down the left-hand side and the Situation, Action and Result along the top. I like to give each example a name as it makes it easier to recall. In the grid, I don't write the complete narrative of my answer (as I have done with the florist example above), just the high-level bullet points that underpin the story. The grid below shows how this might look.

Question	Example Name	Situation	Action	Result
Give us an example of a time when you have had to deal with conflict in the workplace	Evening rotas	• The shop is open until 8 p.m. every day • We had a rota system for who stayed late each day • Some people were very unhappy as they felt that others abused the system to get the shifts they wanted • Caused significant unrest and started to affect staff relationships	• I met with everyone and explained that this needed to be resolved • I then met with each individual to understand their issues • This highlighted two key issues: i. Some people were swapping shifts that they couldn't do ii. Some people actively wanted to do extra shifts	• We created a system that allowed individuals to "post" a shift they either wanted to swap or not do • This gave everyone the same opportunity to swap or pick up extra shifts • Everyone signed up to the system • System working for six months now • Reduced complaints • Improved communication and team togetherness
Give us an example of a time when you have delivered change to a system or organisation	*Name your example*	*Key bullet points to describe the situation*	*Key bullet points to describe **your** actions*	*Key bullet points to describe the results*

Once you've filled up a grid with answers to as many possible "give us an example of" questions as you can think of, go back through your answers and make sure your role is clear. As I said earlier, you should be the hero of your own story. If you're not, then either go back and rewrite it to ensure it focuses on your role, or if you can't honestly write the response in a way that puts you at the centre, ditch this answer and think of one where you are the hero.

A blank copy of the SAR form is available to download at www.howtogethired.co.uk in the documents section.

Chapter Summary

Let's review the key points we have covered in this chapter.

- Behavioural questions are questions that begin with "Give us an example of a time when" (or a variation on this).
- These questions offer you a fantastic chance to showcase your previous experience and tell a story to the panel.
- People often answer these questions poorly as they struggle to articulate the scenario they are describing and the role they played in it.
- Preparing answers for these questions using the SAR – Situation, Actions and Result – structure helps to ensure you get all of the key information across to the panel in a coherent way.
- Once you have developed a number of these responses and recorded them in a SAR grid, you can start to adapt your narrative so you can use it to answer more than one question; for example, you may be able to use the answer you have prepared for the question "Please tell us about a time when you have delivered change to a system or organisation" to answer the question "Please tell us about a time when you have shown leadership in a difficult situation."
- Whatever example you use, it is important to remember that you should be the hero of your own story.

14

PRESENTATIONS

Public speaking is said to be one of the most common fears among adults and giving a presentation is certainly one of the things people find most daunting about the interview process. I've spoken to people who have submitted a fantastic application, been invited to interview, and then pulled out once they are told they will need to give a presentation. However, like nearly everything else in life, presenting is a skill that people can develop through practice and is not something people should be scared of.

Below are a few golden rules for giving a presentation in a job interview.

Rule 1: Answer the Question

All too often people answer the question they would have liked to have been asked, rather than the question that has actually been asked. Therefore, it is really important throughout the process of developing and writing a presentation to check back every so often to make sure you are addressing the specific question being asked.

I would take the title of the presentation you have been given and break it down into sub-questions. Imagine you have been asked to give a presentation entitled "Identify the major internal and external challenges the company will face over the next one to five years, and how you would address them."

This is a typical, overly complex presentation title that a middle or senior manager might expect to see when being invited to interview. Let's break the title apart into a set of more manageable questions.

I would start by translating the time scale they are asking for (one to five years). I read this as covering both the short term (one to two years), and the medium to long term (three to five years). Therefore, you probably need to have two sets of sub-questions for each of the questions in the presentation, which might look something like this.

1. Internal challenges in the short term
2. Internal challenges in the medium/long term
3. External challenges in the short term
4. External challenges in the medium/long term
5. Solutions to internal challenges in the short term
6. Solutions to internal challenges in the medium/long term
7. Solutions to external challenges in the short term
8. Solutions to external challenges in the medium/long term

Now you've got the questions you need to answer clearly

defined, your research and preparation will be a lot more focused. When preparing your presentation, I would suggest pausing at regular intervals and asking yourself the question "Does the content of this presentation actually address one of the sub-questions being asked?"

Rule 2: Conduct Research, Then Selection

Often people use their presentation to share everything they know about a subject, regardless of how relevant it is to the question being asked. One of the key skills most managers like in their employees is the ability to separate the important information from everything else. People who lack confidence in this skill tend to want to share everything with you and let you decide what is significant and what is noise. This can be incredibly frustrating for a manager and makes for a very inefficient employee. For those who have this skill, a presentation is a great opportunity to show that you possess it. For those who don't have it, a presentation is a great opportunity to start to develop it.

When preparing a presentation there are two well-defined stages. Keep them separate and you're onto a winner, but mix them up and you're likely to make life very hard for yourself. These two stages are research and selection. Simply put, research is all your background work, where you gather the information you need, organise your thoughts, and make sure what you have found adequately answers the questions you are being asked. Selection is where you take the information from your research and decide what information is really important and what can be discarded.

I need to emphasise at this point that I am not suggesting

that a lot of the research you do is pointless. The more thorough your research, the more of an understanding you will have of the subject area, and the better prepared you will be. However, every time you cram a piece of insignificant information into your presentation, you increase the chance that your insightful and important comments will go unnoticed. Having this additional information in the back of your mind means that should someone ask a question about a specific point, you have all the details ready to respond.

Rule 3: Content Before Slides

It is not uncommon for someone to give a presentation that they have clearly spent a great deal of time on, with beautiful slides and graphics, but for all the visual brilliance, the content of the presentation is weak. This is usually a result of someone spending a week playing with their slide background and design, making things whizz in and out, and then realising they've got to actually create the content. I am all for a bit of style, but not at the cost of content.

Therefore, I recommend that people develop their presentation using a boring, blank template. Start with a plain white background and black text. Only when you've got the content of your presentation to the point where you are completely happy should you start playing around with your slide formatting. If you've got a slide template you like using, start with the plain template and then import or cut and paste your slides in once you're happy with the text.

Rule 4: The Sandwich Structure

I like to think of a presentation as a sandwich. In the middle you have your filling, which will vary depending on the presentation title, the company, your audience and many other factors. However, that filling sits between two slices of bread that will remain the same regardless. Let's start with the bread.

The bread

These are the first two slides and last two slides and are the foundation of your presentation. They should be as follows.

1. First slide – title page
2. Second slide – content/overview
3. Penultimate slide – summary/conclusion
4. Last slide – thank you and questions

In theory, an interviewer should be able to look at these four slides alone and get a clear sense of who you are and what you're here to talk about (first slide), how you have decided to structure your presentation and the key topic areas you plan to cover (second slide), the most important points you would like the interviewer(s) to take away from your presentation (penultimate slide) and that you are a polite and wonderful person (last slide).

The filling

As you would expect, your filling is the meat of the presentation and the part that will take up the most time. Let's continue using the example above with the presentation title "Identify the major internal and external challenges the company will face over the next one to five years, and how you would address them." We have broken that down into sub-questions which will provide the basis of the presentation structure. Here are those sub-questions again.

1. Internal challenges in the short term
2. Internal challenges in the medium/long term
3. External challenges in the short term
4. External challenges in the medium/long term
5. Solutions to internal challenges in the short term
6. Solutions to internal challenges in the medium/long term
7. Solutions to external challenges in the short term
8. Solutions to external challenges in the medium/long term

Now you need to decide how you are going to structure the answers to those questions in a way that will feel logical and flow nicely.

Rule 5: A Maximum of One Slide Per Minute

The simplest rule of all. Excluding your title and final thank you and questions slide, you should have a maximum of one slide per minute of presentation. So, if you are asked to give a ten-minute presentation, that would be ten slides, including your content/overview slide and your summary/conclusion slide. That means that for the "filling" of your presentation you have eight slides.

Rule 6: Less is More. Slides Are Guides, Not a Script

There is nothing worse than sitting through a presentation where the slides are jam-packed with words, in a font size you can hardly read, and the candidate simply reads the text from the slides verbatim. If you are going to do this, you may as well either not have any slides at all or just give the panel the slides to read and sit yourself quietly in the corner while they read. It is actually really hard to read something yourself at the same time as it is being read to you. Your brain is forced to either read or listen, or more often than not give up and do neither. If you want to test this, try watching television with the subtitles on and the volume turned up loud. Because the dialogue and subtitles are always slightly out of sync, it is very challenging to follow both at the same time.

Good slides act as a guide, highlighting the key points that you are going to address. They should help the audience follow the flow of your presentation by introducing the concept you are talking about. For instance, if your next slide is going to talk about the five most important factors in running a successful ice cream parlour, listing each of the five, together with your justification for each point, it might look like the slide below (please note I know nothing about the ice cream business and this is purely an illustration).

Key Factors for Success

- Location. Somewhere with heavy foot traffic to attract the maximum amount of passers by. Also important to be visible from a long distance away so customers know which way to head.

- A range of products to suit all demographics. Due to the wide range in visitors to seaside areas (from young families to the elderly) it is important that the product range caters to all tastes. There are also many diet friendly products such as dairy free ice creams and gluten free cones.

- Great customer service. The ice cream business is driven by repeat custom and that is gained or lost through customer service. Ensuring that people have a positive interaction with the parlour can significantly increase revenue.

- A reliable supply chain. Having a strong product range is only beneficial if your supply chain means that you always have these products to offer.

- Flexible staffing. Workload is driven by a number of external factors such as the tide times and the weather. Therefore, a workforce that can flex their hours to meet changing demand is critical.

The slide looks cluttered and overwhelming. Because of all the text, the five key points don't stand out and so it is less likely they will be remembered. Below is what the slide looks like when you just include the five points and save the rest for your narrative.

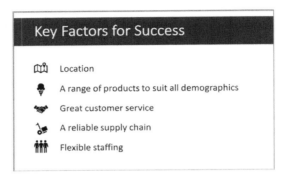

The empty space and bigger font makes the slide much easier on the eye, and allows the panel to quickly scan the slide and then focus their attention on you and what you are saying. Creating the space also allows you to add a few simple icons to make your slide look more attractive.

Rule 7: Practise, Practise, Practise

When it comes to an interview, it is often a step into the unknown. As we looked at earlier, you can make some educated guesses as to what you will be asked and prepare accordingly, but you will never know exactly what questions the panel will throw at you or how the structure of the interview will work. The exception to this is the presentation. For ten glorious minutes (or however long your presentation is), you are in complete control. You control the content, the pace, the atmosphere, and if you ask for people to save their questions until the end, you get to do this without interruption.

This is brilliant because it means you can have as many trial runs as you want. When I am preparing to give a big presentation, whether for an interview, conference or important meeting, I will usually practise it at least ten times. I stand in my office or bedroom with my laptop and deliver the talk over and over again until I can do it without any notes or cue cards. As a general rule, I assume that if someone reads from their notes when giving a presentation, it is because they don't know the content well enough. Your slides should act as your cue cards in case you get stuck, but if you require a script to read from you are simply not prepared.

Unfortunately, many people do not take advantage of this opportunity. All too often, when people deliver their presentation it feels like it is the first time they have done it from start to finish. This is part of the reason so many people overrun on their timing. Once you've practised on your own, give your presentation to trusted friends, family and colleagues to get some honest feedback. If you're feeling really brave, set up your phone to record yourself giving the presentation and then watch it back. This is a great way to get a true sense of what your audience will see.

Rule 8: Keep to Time

I am always amazed by people's inability to follow simple instructions when it comes to presentations. Setting someone a specific time limit is a very easy way to test not just a candidate's timekeeping skills, but also their ability to follow instructions. If I ask you to give a seven-minute presentation, then I want you to give a seven-minute presentation. People seem to interpret a clear instruction like this as "I'd like you to give a presentation that is about seven minutes long, but anything between five minutes and 15 minutes will be fine." Worse still is when people comment on their own poor timekeeping during their presentation, saying things like "I realise that I'm probably way over on time, but I'll rush through these last eight slides." This tells the panel that you are fully aware of your poor time management, and yet you haven't seen fit to do anything about it.

Some people on interview panels are more tolerant than others. Personally, if I've asked you to give a seven-minute presentation, and you get to seven minutes, unless you're just finishing your last slide I will ask you to stop. This means that if you've got some amazing content on your last few slides, the panel will never get to hear it.

Chapter Summary

Let's review the key points we have covered in this chapter.

- Public speaking is something many people fear. However, the combination of a small amount of understanding about how to deliver presentations, together with some focused practice, can turn even the most nervous candidates into confident presenters.
- The first mistake candidates tend to make is not answering the question the presentation title asks. Often people answer the question they would have liked to have been asked instead. The trick to avoiding this is to check back throughout your

research, preparation and practice to ensure the content of your presentation answers the question the panel has set.

- When preparing a presentation there is a temptation to start with your slides. People often waste a huge amount of time playing with slide structure, fiddling with colours and backgrounds, before they have actually decided on the content of their presentation. You should start with research and selection of the information you are going to use, and only put them into slide format once you are happy with the content.

- Presentations should start with a title slide, followed by a content or overview slide, and end with a summary slide, followed by a final thank you and questions slide. In between these two sets of slides comes the content of your presentation.

- You should present at a speed of one slide per minute, no faster.

- Slides should show the high-level points you are making in your presentation. They should not contain the entire content or reflect your script.

- The biggest secret to delivering an amazing presentation is practice. If you practise your presentation ten times or more you should be able to do it from memory, without the need for notes or cue cards.

- Stick to the time limit you are given by the panel to show you can follow instructions and are respectful of people's time.

PART IV

INTERVIEWING FOR YOUR DREAM JOB

"Hide not your talents, they for use were made; what's a sundial in the shade?"

- Benjamin Franklin

After all your diligent preparation for your interview, you should be in a great position to impress the panel with your expertise, experience, communication skills and knowledge. In this section of the book, we will first take a look behind the scenes of job interviews to give you a sense of how the process works and what you can do to maximise your chances of success. We will then look at how to avoid some of the biggest pitfalls of interviews. Finally, we will focus on communication skills, and how to interpret the interview panel's verbal and non-verbal cues.

15

INTERVIEWING: BEHIND THE SCENES

I f you've never had the opportunity to sit on an interview panel before, you may well wonder what happens when the candidates aren't in the room, how interview panels are structured and, most importantly, how panels make decisions. Hopefully this chapter will help answer these questions for you.

I must start by saying that there are lots of ways of conducting interviews, and this will vary depending on the organisation recruiting, the type and level of job they are interviewing for, and the level of experience of the person responsible for the recruitment. However, the basics should remain much the same regardless.

How Panels Are Structured

Most interview panels have a chair. The chair is usually either the person who will be line managing the new employee or the most senior person on the panel. It is important you know who the chair is, as they will have the final say on who gets hired. They should be pretty easy to spot, as they will be the person who makes the introductions at the start and explains the structure of the interview. Alongside the chair you will normally have one or more people who work within the department (including the line manager of the post if they aren't the chair). Depending on the level of job, you may also have someone from the HR department and/or someone independent. These days interview panels are supposed to be gender neutral, so you are likely to have a mix of men and women.

If the interview panel members are professional and organised, then prior to the day of the interview they will have worked out the questions they plan to ask. If not, this may be done in the half an hour prior to the first candidate entering the room. In order to make interviews as fair as possible, the same questions should be asked to all the candidates, so everyone has the same opportunity to shine (or shoot themselves in the foot). Usually, the same members of the interview panel will ask the same questions, in the same order, to each candidate, which just helps to simplify the process.

The panel will get together before the first interview, run through the questions, tweaking them if necessary and agreeing who is going to ask what. This is usually followed by a brief discussion about the candidates. Depending on the size of the panel, there is likely to be a mix of two groups of people. The first group are those who were involved in the shortlisting process. This person or people will have read all the applications during the candidate selection process and so will be familiar with each of the candidates and may well have a preference for a certain candidate already (we will discuss why this is so important shortly). The second group are those who were not involved in short-listing. These people may have had a chance to look at the applications for the candidates on the interview list prior to the interviews, but if they have done so it is unlikely to have been in any depth. As a result, the people in group two tend to come into the process with a more open mindset.

As I mentioned above, the people who have been involved in the shortlisting are likely to come into the interview stage with preconceived opinions of the candidates. This is a really important point to understand for two reasons. Firstly, the people who are involved in shortlisting are usually the people who are responsible for recruiting the individual (the hiring manager or chair of the panel) and therefore their opinions really count for something. Secondly, it is human nature to want to be proved right, to the extent that we often see and hear what we want to in order to reach the conclusion we were hoping for. Often, after shortlisting, a manager will have one candidate in mind who they feel is the front runner. This is usually, but not always, the candidate that scored highest during the shortlisting process or the candidate that made the effort to speak to the manager prior to the interview. After expressing their excitement about this candidate either to other people on the panel or just to themselves, they develop an attachment to that candidate, almost like they've placed an emotional or professional bet on that person. From that point on they tend to treat that individual with a positive bias. This can be played out in many different ways, but a good example is providing positive feedback to the candidate during the interview when they finish answering a question, for example "thank you very much, that was a really good answer". This has a number of effects that benefit the candidate. It boosts their confidence, and it can influence other panel members who pick up on the positive cues and remember that the candidate gave a very good answer to that question (regardless of if they did or not).

I can imagine at this point you are reading this and thinking, that's really unfair! I don't disagree with you. The interview process is supposed to be unbiased, with each candidate treated in the same way. However, as we all know, life isn't fair. The important thing to realise, given this knowledge, is that it is worth you doing everything you can to be the candidate the hiring manager is rooting for. The better your application, and the more effort you've made to interact with the people recruiting you, the more chance you have of being someone's preferred candidate and benefiting from this unconscious bias.

Scoring

Usually the panel will have some sort of scoring sheet. There are a number of ways these sheets are formatted. Some have each of the questions that the candidates are going to be asked, and for each question there is a section for the interviewer to make notes and then a box for them to write their score for that specific question. Others produce a grid with the criteria listed in the personal specification and an associated score box or checkbox for each one. The method and structure of the scoring doesn't really matter, so long as it is consistent for each candidate. At the end of the interviews, each panel member will total up the scores so they can compare across candidates.

What I have described above is how the system should work and is a very fair and equitable way of defining who is the best candidate. I'm sure by now you can see there is a "but" coming. As I described earlier, members of interview panels are human beings and are susceptible to the same bias as the rest of us. Finding the right candidate is as much of an art as it is a science, and that makes it very difficult to be governed solely by a rigid scoring structure (based on merit). Often people will find reasons to give points to a candidate they like which they might withhold for a candidate they're not so taken with.

In Chapter 19, we will talk about how the scores are used to help support the final decision-making of who to hire.

Chapter Summary

Let's review the key points we have covered in this chapter.

- Interview panels are usually chaired by either the person who will be responsible for managing the new employee or the most senior member of the panel. This will be the person who makes the ultimate decision about who gets hired.
- Some of the panel members will have been involved in shortlisting and so will have some familiarity with the candidate, while others will have little or no prior knowledge.
- Panels will often include a member of the HR team or an external person to ensure the process is fair. This is common for more senior positions.

- The panel should ask the same questions in the same order for each of the candidates. This ensures that each candidate gets the same opportunity to impress.
- Most interview panels will develop a rough scoring system to help compare the candidates.

16

THINK BEFORE YOU SPEAK. THE BATTLE OF BRAIN AND MOUTH

In its most basic form, an interview is simply you answering lots of questions, and asking a few yourself. Answering questions is something we've all been doing hundreds of times a day since we started school, and therefore most people assume it is something they are naturally good at and can do without much thought. However, the vast majority of questions we answer in our daily lives have a limited number of responses, and our answers don't usually require an explanation (e.g. yes or no). Answering questions in an interview is a completely different skill set, and from experience I would say that it is a skill that many people need to develop further.

One of the major differences between answering questions in everyday life and in an interview is the thought process. Many of the questions we normally answer don't require our conscious thought process to kick in, we just intuitively find the answer. Compare this with an interview question, where you are likely to need to consider and formulate your answer before giving it.

Training yourself to take the time to think of an answer before you start talking is the simplest way to improve your interview performance, and with very little effort, the results can be staggering. When helping someone prepare for an interview, I often ask them a question and let them start talking straight away. When they get to the end of their answer, they usually know they have just spouted a load of rubbish. We will then repeat the exercise, but this time they are not allowed to start talking until they have thought about their answer for at least 10 seconds. The second answer is always infinitely better than the first. Most people assume that sitting there in silence, with an interview panel all staring at you, would be so awkward that they would never consider doing it. However, I can say from experience that I would much rather a candidate takes their time to answer than talks for the sake of talking. It is not nearly as awkward as you may think.

When a candidate starts to talk before formulating their answer, one of three things tends to happen. I call these the U-turn, the white flag and, worst of all, the tangent trap. Here is how these three scenarios usually arise.

The interviewer asks a question. The candidate smiles, nods politely and then launches into their response. After a few seconds a pained look starts to spread across the candidate's face as their brain realises that it's not really sure where it is planning to go with this answer. The candidate's brain realises that it just needs a few seconds to get its thoughts in order, but the mouth is in mid-sentence and doesn't seem to be showing any signs of stopping. As that sentence comes to an end the brain sees an opportunity. If it can just get the mouth to talk about something, anything, related to the subject at hand, just for a few seconds, it can get back on track with answering the question the interviewer asked. The brain finds something vaguely suitable for the mouth to talk about while it formulates its plan. The mouth gratefully accepts the task and gets to work. As the brain works on what it wants to talk about, it can't help but overhear what the mouth is saying. This is where we reach the point of the three possible scenarios.

The U-Turn. This is the best outcome of the three. As the mouth is talking, the brain is hit by a wave of inspiration and the answer to the interviewer's question begins to formulate itself. The brain, realising that the mouth is about to wander down the dark path of a tangent, takes control and wraps up whatever rubbish the mouth is spouting, and steers the narrative back to answering the question at hand.

The White Flag. This is the rarest of the three outcomes. As the brain is searching for inspiration, it can't help but listen to the twaddle that the mouth is sharing with the people it is so desperate to impress. Finally, the brain decides that enough is enough and it raises the white flag. It stops the mouth in its tracks and instructs it to tell the interviewer that unfortunately it has lost its train of thought and asks whether it would be possible to start over.

The Tangent Trap. This is by far the most common outcome. Like in the white flag, the brain cannot help but listen to what the mouth is saying. While the brain's focus is definitely on searching for the answer to the question posed by the interviewer, it starts to pay a bit more attention to what the mouth is saying. Soon the brain's focus shifts to helping the mouth to continue its current subject line, the original question now all but forgotten. The brain and the mouth continue to work together as they sleepwalk further and further into the tangent trap. At some point, when the brain and the mouth start to run out of things to add to the tangent, the brain suddenly wakes, looks around at where the monologue has led to and says "How on earth did I get here?" At this point the brain tells the mouth to trail off the sentence and then try and smile as confidently as possible at the interviewer in the hope of giving the impression that it has just delivered an insightful and concise answer to the question.

If you ever find yourself in this situation the option that I, and I think most interviewers, prefer is the white flag. I like people who have the guts to say "Wow, I'm really not sure where I was going with that answer. Sorry about that. Would you mind repeating the question and I'll start again?" Firstly, you will gain my respect by admitting you got it wrong. Secondly, you won't waste the opportunity to answer the question well. However, the best tactic of all is to avoid all three, by thinking before you speak.

Chapter Summary

Let's review the key points we have covered in this chapter.

- Most people who struggle to answer questions in interviews do so not because they don't know the answer, but because they are unable to think logically and articulate their thoughts.
- Like most things, answering questions in an interview is a skill that can be developed with preparation and practice.
- The biggest mistake people make is not taking the time to construct their answer before they start

speaking. They assume that a period of silence while they think about what they are going to say will be incredibly awkward and thus start their answer the moment the person asking the question finishes.

- There is nothing wrong with pausing after you have been asked a question. If you're worried that this will seem awkward, then ask the panel for a few seconds to think about your answer. This will be seen as a sign of maturity and confidence, not a weakness.

- Not taking time to consider your answer before you start speaking usually ends up with you losing the thread of your answers, often forgetting the original questions you were asked.

- If you find yourself losing the thread of what you are saying, or that you have wandered into a tangent that has little or nothing to do with the question you have been asked, stop talking, apologise to the panel, and ask if you can start over. Again, this will be seen as a sign of maturity and self-awareness.

17

READ YOUR AUDIENCE

As you've heard me say many times by now, this isn't all about you. Your job during an interview is to keep me and my fellow panel members happy, entertained, interested, intrigued and above all rooting for you. By far the best way to see how you're doing is to take a look at our body language. Once again, reading this you are probably thinking "well yeah, that's pretty obvious". Well, yes, it should be. Yet time after time, I sit in interviews listening to candidates drone on, looking at my colleagues on the interview panel who are showing very unsubtle signs of boredom, irritation, anguish and even despair, and yet the candidate continues as if we're all hanging off their every word.

Therefore, being able to read both verbal and non-verbal cues is a massive advantage when being interviewed. It's much broader than just identifying when you've gone on too long with an answer. At every point during an interview, you can gain clues from the interviewers as to how you're doing. There are a number of great books on the subject.

One of my favourites is *What Every BODY is Saying: An Ex-FBI Agent's Guide to Speed-Reading People* by Joe Navarro. As the title suggests, the author spent many years interrogating people for the FBI and has done a great job of explaining how to read people's cues.

Negative Cues

Let's start with the negative. Below is a list of the common verbal and non-verbal cues to tell you that you've lost the interviewer's interest, they don't like what you're saying, or they are unlikely to offer you the job.

1. **Classic signs of boredom.** These include yawning, fidgeting, massaging their face or hands, leaning back from the table, reduced eye contact or glazed eyes.
2. **Reading while you're answering a question.** Picking up bits of paper in front of them and reading (this is usually a sign they've lost interest in you and are looking at the CV of the next candidate).
3. **A lack of a smile.** Most people, even the grumpiest of individuals, will give a polite smile when asking a question and listening to a response. A constant blank expression usually means you need to win the individual over.
4. **Body position.** Turning their body away from you, especially if they turn their body towards the door (this is an unconscious move people make when they want to be elsewhere).
5. **A lack of follow-up questions or a very quick interview.** This could be a sign that you're nailing

every question; however, it is more likely that the panel have lost interest in your answers and simply want to get to the end of the interview as soon as possible.

6. **A lack of "selling" of the job or company.** When you really like a candidate, you make an effort to sell the job and the organisation they will be working for throughout the interview. If they make no effort to do this, you may be losing them.

7. **Repetition of positive words.** When people aren't really listening but want to look like they are, they tend to overplay their engagement by repeatedly saying things like "Yes, I see, yes, very interesting, yes, yes." Contrast this with when someone is actually actively listening, when most of their cues are non-verbal.

8. **When the interviewers seem a bit confused as to who's asking the next question.** Usually the panel will decide before the interview who is going to ask what questions and in what order. If there is confusion about who is supposed to be asking the next question, it can be a sign that one of the panel members has decided to skip their question as they want to move things along.

9. **Interruptions.** Ideally in an interview, the panel member will ask a question, the interviewee will answer it, and then the panel members may ask a follow-up question if necessary. If a panel member feels the need to interrupt you while you're giving an answer, it usually means one of three things. Firstly, you are taking too long with your answer. Secondly, you seem to have lost the thread of your answer and the panel members don't have a clue

what you're talking about. Finally, you have said something that is so provocative (this could be in either a good or bad way) that the panel member feels they need to interject (more on interruptions shortly).

10. **They highlight negative aspects of the job.** This is a classic unconscious way of both trying to put a candidate you don't like off and trying to expose their flaws.

11. **Lack of next steps.** Usually an interview ends with a bunch of logistical questions and information, such as asking what's the best number to contact you on or if offered the job, when could you start. If you don't get asked any of these questions, then there is probably a reason why!

Positive Cues

The vast majority of the positive cues are simply the opposite of the negative cues, so I am not going to list them all. However, a few positive cues are worth mentioning briefly.

1. **Leaning in.** When people are interested and engaged they tend to lean forward towards the person they are engaging with.

2. **Nodding.** I tend to nod along when a candidate is on the right track with a question.

3. **Asking specific follow-up questions.** If a panel member has a question about something you said in your previous answer then it means they were actually listening to your answer, which is always a positive sign.

4. **Overtly positive comments.** When an interviewer

goes above and beyond just thanking you for your
answer to say how interesting or insightful it is.

5. **When you spark a debate.** When you make a
comment in your answer that other panel members
comment on and then start to debate among
themselves. This is a sign that you've said
something they haven't heard before.

6. **Laughing.** A jovial atmosphere among the panel is
usually a sign that people are enjoying your
company and are not in a hurry to end the
interview.

How to Interpret Interruptions

If a candidate has been going on for too long with an answer
and a panel member decides to interrupt them, they will
usually start off subtly in the hope that the candidate will
catch on, and then get more unsubtle if their initial attempts
are ignored. There are three basic ways to signal to a candidate to stop.

1. **Non-verbal interruptions.** If someone is going on
too long with their answer most panel members
will start with non-verbal cues to try and signal to
the interviewee to stop. If this fails, they will move
on to using verbal cues.

2. **Polite interruptions.** These usually take the form
of positive comments, like "thank you" or "very
thorough", together with non-verbal cues signalling
they have heard enough.

3. **Firm interruptions.** If despite subtle non-verbal
cues, followed by polite interruptions, followed by
unsubtle non-verbal cues the candidate is still not

getting the hint, most people will move to much firmer interruptions to bring the answer to an end. For example, they may say "I'm afraid I'm going to have to stop you there as I'm very conscious of the time." If you get this kind of interruption during an interview, you need to make a mental note to keep your answers concise for the rest of the interview. Being asked to stop more than once is probably a clear signal that you won't be offered the job.

It is really important that you look for the signs of a non-verbal interruption and respond accordingly. It is also good to keep track of how many times you've been interrupted. If it has happened more than a few times, then you need to consider a change of tactics. Clearly your answers are too long, so consider giving shorter answers and then asking a clarification question at the end of your answers, such as "Does that answer your question, or would you like more explanation?"

Interview Timing

As I have already mentioned, and will discuss in greater detail later in this section of the book, keeping to time during an interview is really important. Presentations are the most obvious manifestation of this, as you are usually given a specific amount of time. However, it is important to consider the overall time you have as part of your interview. Both you and the interview panel should share the same goal of getting through the pre-amble, presentation or exercise (if there is one), interview questions, your questions, and the closing comments within a given time window.

The interview panel will all know what this time window is, and they will work hard to keep to it as they likely have another five people they need to interview that day. You, on the other hand, may not have a clue how much time has been set aside for your interview. Candidates who understand that the panel don't have all day and keep their responses to a sensible length will automatically score some points with the interviewers. However, the reverse is also true. I like to keep to time when interviewing, so if a candidate gives very long-winded answers to even the simplest questions early on, and my attempts to curtail them have failed, I will be forced to try and make up time later on. This might be by me (or other panel members) having to cut a candidate off part way through an answer, it might be by rephrasing questions so they require a short answer or, worst of all, it might be by skipping over some questions. When any of these happen, you lose the opportunity to sell yourself. Unfortunately, it will probably be that the one question you were desperately hoping for, and had the perfect answer for, is the one that gets missed in order to finish the interview on time.

To help you better understand how much time you have, try and work out what the interview schedule is. If you are offered more than one time slot when you are invited for interview, use the time between slots as the basis, then subtract 10 minutes for the panel to chat, read through the next candidate's documents, etc. If interviews are 45 minutes apart, assume that they will want to talk to you for a maximum of 35 minutes. Keep this in mind during your interview.

Chapter Summary

Let's review the key points we have covered in this chapter.

- Throughout an interview the panel will give you both verbal and non-verbal cues as to how you are doing. Being able to read and interpret these cues will allow you to adjust your delivery during the interview.
- Negative cues, such as yawning or fidgeting, blank facial expressions, negative body positions or a lack of follow-up questions, should tell you that you are losing the panel's attention. In these situations, it might be that you are giving very long answers to simple questions or not actually answering the questions being asked.
- Positive cues, such as leaning forward, active nodding, detailed follow-up questions and laughter, are all signs that the interview is going well.
- If a panel member feels the need to interrupt a candidate, this is generally a bad sign. Most interviewers will start with subtle non-verbal interruptions if a candidate is talking too much or giving incoherent answers. If this fails, they will move to polite interruptions and finally firm interruptions. If you find yourself being interrupted, you need to make a mental note of it and adapt the way you answer questions accordingly. Having to interrupt a candidate more than a couple of times during an interview is a sure sign that the candidate will not be hired.

PART V

THE OUTCOME

"There is no failure. Only feedback."

- Robert Allen

You'll leave your interview with a sense of how you got on, but inevitably the wait to find out if you've been successful can be a stressful period. In this section of the book, we'll look at the factors outside your control that may influence who gets the job, how interview panels make selection decisions, negotiating a job offer, and receiving post-interview feedback.

18

IT'S OUT OF YOUR HANDS

B y now I hope you've understood the basic premise that there is an awful lot you can do to prepare yourself for an interview and therefore increase your chances of success. However, there are a number of factors that fall outside your control. My intention is not to try and scare you or depress your new-found optimism for job interviews, but to give you an insight into what happens in interview rooms up and down the country every day.

Here's the theory that stands behind good interview practice. The process should be fair and equitable, giving each candidate the same opportunity to communicate why they are the best person for the job. The interviewers should not be influenced by any personal views or beliefs that may discriminate against a candidate or multiple candidates.

Most organisations now have very well-developed diversity training packages to ensure that discriminatory behaviour does not take place. In addition, candidates should all be asked the same questions in an interview, and be asked to complete the same assessed activities (e.g. presentations or tests). This helps to ensure that everyone is given an equitable platform to sell themselves.

While these measures go a long way to delivering equality in the interview process, the reality is that interviews are conducted by human beings and are therefore subject to our common flaws. Below are two examples of behaviours, which I am guilty of myself, to illustrate the elements of the interview process that you will not be able to control.

Timing

Like most people, when I'm hungry or tired I tend to lose a bit of focus and get a bit grumpy. If you're the first candidate of the day, when I'm fuelled with coffee and enthusiasm, you will meet a slightly different version of me to the one interviewing the last candidate before lunch or the final candidate at the end of a full day of interviewing. Each candidate will be asked the same questions and given the same opportunities; however, my patience for your long, rambling answers is likely to be a little shorter if you stand between me and the steak and stilton sandwich I've been thinking about off and on for the last 30 minutes.

If you think this is unbelievably unfair, and that professional people shouldn't behave in such a way, let me share with you a great illustration of how this behaviour influences far more serious situations than a job interview. In his book *The One Thing*, Gary Keller explores some research done at Stanford Business School to understand the impact of willpower (or lack of it) on parole hearings in Israel. The research followed eight judges over a ten-month period, and looked at the decisions they made (to either grant or refuse parole) at different times of the day. The judges worked long days with only two breaks: a morning snack break and a lunch break. The researchers found that if you were lucky enough to be the prisoner in front of the judge directly after either the snack or lunch break, you had a 65% chance of being released. However, if you were the prisoner directly before a break or at the end of the day, your chance of release was nearly zero.

So be thankful that your future freedom doesn't rest on my blood sugar level! On a serious note, as I assume I am not the only person who suffers from this sort of loss of willpower, if I am offered a choice of interview slots I will always take the one as close to the start of the day, or after an obvious lunch break if possible.

Other Candidates

When being interviewed you are not only being compared to other candidates, but you are also able to influence our views of other candidates. If you have the misfortune of being the person who follows a strong candidate that the panel really likes, you will have to work a lot harder and perform better to impress us. Likewise, if you follow a flop who has just wasted half an hour of the panel's precious time, it will be a lot easier for you to leave the interview with the panel praising your competence and communication skills.

I spoke to someone recently who was on a panel with a very experienced hiring manager. The first candidate performed very well and was liked by all on the panel. As soon as the first candidate had left the room, the hiring manager started to go through the CV of the second candidate, pointing out reasons why the second candidate was inferior. His mind was pretty much made up before the second candidate even stepped through the door.

Internal Candidates and Forgone Conclusions

One of the downsides of the very HR-driven, anti-discriminatory practices employed in the UK (to be clear I believe there are many upsides which outweigh the downsides) is that managers are often forced to enter a recruitment process when there is no need to do so. A good example of this is where someone is moving to a new post and they have a deputy who has been developed to take over when the senior person leaves as part of a succession planning process. It might be that everyone in the organisation has known for the last year that person X would be leaving or retiring, and that person Y was being trained to take over the role. Despite this, many organisations will not feel comfortable simply promoting person Y to the role, for fear of being challenged as anti-competitive. As a result, the job will have to go out to advert, and a recruitment process will need to take place that is highly likely to result in person Y being hired (especially if the organisation has invested a lot in developing person Y for the role). Everyone within the organisation will know this is pretty much a done deal; however, you, the external candidate who happened to see the job advert on the website, for the one day it was posted, will have no clue. You will apply, put in a great application that ticks all the boxes, and so they will have no choice but to interview you, despite having no intention of hiring you for the post.

In my mind this is a colossal waste of time. It is hugely frustrating from the perspective of the hiring manager, and unfair on the candidates who put their heart and soul into an application and interview when they stand little or no chance of success.

I could list a dozen more examples but I think you get the point. There are a whole bunch of things that you can't control, which makes it all the more important that you put the time and effort into managing those things you can control. If you've done everything you can to prepare for an interview, but events conspire against you, or there was just a better candidate on the day, you can hold your head high and mark it down as an experience.

Chapter Summary

Let's review the key points we have covered in this chapter.

- While there is a huge amount you can do to increase your chances of success, sometimes factors outside your control mean that someone else will get the job.
- It is important to understand that not getting the job doesn't always mean that you have failed.
- While the interview process is supposed to be designed and delivered in a standardised way that gives every candidate the same opportunity, unfortunately this is often not the case.
- Many of the external factors that may affect your prospects are the result of normal human biases and flaws, such as the mood of the members on the interview panel. An interviewer might read an email or get an urgent message between candidates

which drastically alters their mood. While panel members try to be professional at all times, it is naïve to think that this change in mood will not affect the way they interview the next candidate compared to the last.

- Sometimes jobs are advertised with specific candidates in mind, such as an internal candidate who is being prepared for the role. Even if you deliver the performance of your life in the interview, it may still not be enough to get you the job.

19

CANDIDATE SELECTION: BEHIND THE SCENES

Once all the candidates have been interviewed, the panel will meet (either in person or virtually) to make its decision. This usually starts by eliminating the un-appointable candidates. In my experience this happens pretty quickly, and people tend to find a consensus view on who definitely shouldn't get the job. Occasionally there is a difference of opinion, with one or more members of the panel making the case for a candidate, and depending on the strength of their argument (or their persuasive powers), they might manage to get the candidate to the next stage.

Once the un-appointable candidates (those the panel feel did not meet the requirements of the job) are removed, the discussion turns to those who are left. These are classed as the appointable candidates, which translates as "you've met the basic criteria for the job and so we could appoint you to the position". However, just because you have shown that you possess the qualifications, skills and experience required for the role, it doesn't mean that you are necessarily right for the job.

Usually at this point the chair will go through the candidates one by one, giving their view and then asking others to share their thoughts. These discussions tend to go one of two ways at this point. If there is clearly a preferred candidate, then group think kicks in and people start to reinforce each other's opinions, meaning that a consensus is reached quickly. Alternatively, if the panel is split, with some favouring one candidate and others preferring another, discussions can be long and often heated.

If a panel is split, the final decision will usually be made by the person who will be responsible for managing the individual (who will usually be acting as the chair of the panel). As I mentioned earlier, the key question this person will be asking themselves is "Which of the appointable candidates will make my life easiest?" I can't emphasise this enough. At this point it's not about qualifications, skills or experience, it's about personalities.

Often a candidate can look great on paper, have the qualifications, skills and experience that the panel members are looking for, but just not be the right fit for the position. Unfortunately, this is usually intangible, and so is very hard to quantify or justify. It is not uncommon for one, several, or all members of a panel to express a feeling about a candidate, either positive or negative, that is strong enough to override both the factual information about the individual and their performance on the day.

I would even go as far as saying that the majority of the worst hiring decisions I have made during my career have been when I have hired someone that ticked all the boxes, despite a feeling that they weren't quite the right person for the job.

Likewise, sometimes you are faced with a candidate who clearly isn't the best of the bunch, based on their CV, application or answers in the interview, but there is something about them that makes you want to hire them above other candidates. It might be that the hirer sees the potential for their development in the long term or feels that they would be a perfect fit for the staff already in the team. Sometimes even when a candidate gives incorrect answers to interview questions due to a lack of knowledge or experience, the hirer can see (and be impressed with) their thought process in the way they reach their answer.

The end result is that the panel will identify who their first choice is. They will then turn to the remaining "appointable" candidates and decide who is the second choice or reserve. Occasionally there might even be a third choice, but in my experience that is rare.

The Offer

The next thing that will be decided is what the hiring organisation is willing to offer the preferred candidate. Sometimes this is a decision made by the panel, but often it is left to the chair, manager or budget holder. There are four main drivers that influence this decision:

1. How good is the preferred candidate?
2. Is there one or more reserve candidates?
3. How good are the reserve candidates compared to the first choice?
4. What are the consequences of not appointing?

Imagine there's a fantastic first choice, but no appointable candidates on the reserve list and the job being filled is for a specific project that can't go ahead until someone is in post. In this situation a recruiting manager is likely to be willing to make a lot of concessions on salary, holiday entitlement, working hours, etc. in order to secure their preferred candidate.

Now imagine a scenario where the organisation is recruiting for a position in a pool of secretaries. There are a number of appointable candidates and it was difficult choosing which of them was going to be the first choice. In this situation, there are good backup options, and even if nobody was recruited, it would probably not have a massive impact on the organisation. As a result, the recruiting manager is likely to be a lot less flexible in terms of the offer and their willingness to negotiate.

Once the panel has come to its decision, it is time to pick up the phone and contact the candidates. This can be split into two parts: contacting the candidates that were deemed not to be appointable and breaking the bad news, and contacting the preferred candidate to make a job offer.

Un-Appointable Candidates

As I mentioned above, the un-appointable candidates are those that didn't meet the requirements to fulfil the job. That means that even if the first, second and third choice candidates all turn down the post, the hiring manager would go back out to advert rather than offer it to other candidates interviewed. Some organisations allow someone from their HR team to ring the candidates that are not going to be made an offer (or worse email them) to deliver the bad news. In my view this is bad form. I believe that if someone has gone to the effort to apply for a post and come for an interview, the least the hiring manager can do is show them the respect of contacting them directly. I usually get this out of the way first as I don't like to make people suffer for longer than they have to. We will discuss how I like to deliver the bad news, and how you should respond to it, shortly, in Chapter 21.

Appointable Candidates

If contacting the un-appointable candidates is the sour part of the process, then contacting the successful candidate is most definitely the sweet part. Many recruiting managers like to sleep on things to make sure they've made the right decision. This is especially true if it has been a hard decision to make (either between two or more great candidates, or if the hiring manager is not 100% sure the person about to be offered the job to is right for the post). In my experience, I struggle to recall anyone who has made a decision to appoint a candidate, slept on it overnight, and changed their mind the next day.

That said, like many recruiters, at the end of an interview I will usually tell candidates that they will be contacted the following day (assuming that all the candidates are being interviewed on that day). The reason for this is if I make an offer to my first-choice candidate, and they ask to think about it overnight, and then call the next morning to tell me they have decided not to take the job, I can call my second choice and offer them the job. Because I told them I would be contacting them the following day anyway, they are likely to assume that they were in fact the first-choice candidate. This is important for a couple of reasons. Firstly, it helps to boost their confidence. Nobody likes to think they were the second choice. Secondly, as I mentioned above in the section about deciding how much you are willing to offer a candidate, I don't want the candidate to know they are my backup option as it strengthens their negotiating position and weakens mine.

Chapter Summary

Let's review the key points we have covered in this chapter.

- Once the interviews are all complete, candidates will be designated as either appointable or un-appointable.
- Appointable candidates are those who have met the basic criteria of the post, and the panel are satisfied that they could do the job if appointed.
- Un-appointable candidates are those who have not met the basic criteria. This means that even if all the appointable candidates turn the job down, the panel would still not consider offering these candidates the job.
- Once the appointable candidates have been identified, the panel will then discuss each one in turn. At the end of the discussion the candidates will be ranked, with the best candidate being the first choice. These decisions often become less about the individual's credentials and more about their personalities.

- The first-choice candidate will usually get called first with an offer of the job. The second (and sometimes third) choice candidate will not get called until the first choice has either accepted or rejected the position.

20

RECEIVING A JOB OFFER

Congratulations, you've just received that wonderful call (or possibly face-to-face meeting if you're an internal employee) offering you the job. "Thanks," I hear you say, "but why would you need advice on accepting a job?" you ask. The answer is simple. You have put so much time and effort into getting to a position of being offered the job, it is worth investing a little more effort to ensure you get the best outcome possible. As we will discuss below, a phone call offering you a job does not mean you are guaranteed the job. Therefore, it is important to stay focused and make sure you seal the deal.

Types of Job Offer

There are two main types of job offer and it is important to understand the difference between the two.

1. Conditional job offer: This is usually the offer you get when someone rings you up to offer you the job. It can also be known as an informal offer. As the name would suggest, a conditional offer is an offer that is contingent on you meeting a number of criteria. These might be related to reference checks, background checks (such as Disclosure and Barring Service), occupational health assessments, proof of qualifications or any other criteria that are required for the job. The conditional offer is also reliant on the two parties (the candidate and organisation doing the hiring) finding common ground in terms of compensation and other benefits.

Conditional offers are usually made verbally initially, and put in writing later. This makes it far easier for a company to withdraw, an important point to remember.

2. Unconditional job offer: This is the formal offer that is made in writing. As the name suggests, the offer is not dependent on anything: the job is yours. Once this formal offer is made, it is difficult for an organisation to change their mind.

Preparing to Negotiate

This is probably the part of the whole process that people give the least amount of thought to, but is actually one of the most important steps. Knowing how to respond to a job offer shows that you are both a professional and prepared. Not knowing, on the other hand, can make you look unprofessional, something that might cause the person offering you the post to have second thoughts. Often people don't like to start thinking about how they might act if they receive a job offer as it seems presumptuous at that point; however, without preparation, you will put yourself at a massive disadvantage should you find yourself in a negotiation. Here are my key tips for preparing to negotiate a job offer:

1. Be clear on what you are willing to accept before you start negotiating. The exercise in Chapter 1 should have given you a good idea of what you're willing to accept. It is worth going back to that and having a look at what you wrote. However, having gone through the recruitment process you may have revised your criteria based on how excited you are about the job, company or people you would be working with. Therefore, it will be helpful to either amend your original criteria or complete the exercise again with the specific job in mind (a blank copy of the exercise is available at www.howtogethired.co.uk). Either way, the important thing is to have a clear, honest set of criteria written down to guide you during your negotiations.

2. Be clear on your prioritisation. Once you have a clear idea of what you want, you need to think about your priorities as this will help you to structure the way you negotiate. There are likely to be things that are non-negotiable for you. This could be related to salary or the fact that you want to be able to drop your kids at school three mornings a week so would need to start at 9.30 a.m. on those days. There will be other things that would be nice, but are not essential to you, such as private healthcare insurance. These are the things that you will be willing to compromise on in order to get your higher priorities.

People who enter into a negotiation with a long shopping list of demands end up getting very little (or none) of what they want as it makes it very hard for the other party in the negotiation to understand their key drives. People who have a clear focus on what is important to them are far more likely to walk away happy.

3. Understand the position of the person you are negotiating with. Depending on the sector you are applying for jobs in, your scope for negotiation will vary. It is important to understand the context of the organisation and therefore what you are likely to be able to negotiate on. For example, if you are applying for jobs with the NHS, the employment structures are very rigid. Salaries are structured in bands, with a number of incremental points from the bottom of the band to the top. If you are new to the NHS or moving from a lower band, you will usually start at the bottom of whatever band the job is advertised at, and there will be little scope for negotiation. Annual leave is also very prescriptive, with your allocation dependent on how many years of continuous NHS service you have. Therefore, your scope for negotiation on your basic package (salary, leave, benefits) is very limited. However, the NHS is far more amenable to things like flexible working and study leave than most organisations, and offers great pensions and longer-term benefits. Contrast this with a company in the finance sector, where salary, bonuses and benefits will all be on the table for negotiation, but flexible working or longer-term provisions may not be.

Negotiating a Job Offer

Once you know what it is you want, and have an understanding of the context of the organisation you are negotiating with, you are in a position to negotiate. As negotiations go, they don't come more simple than getting hired, so you don't need to be an expert. However, if you feel the need to become a power negotiator, I would recommend the seminal book *Getting to Yes*, by William Ury and Roger Fisher, which is a brilliant and easy read.

Here are some tips about how to tackle the negotiation itself:

1. **Express your enthusiasm.** Make sure you respond positively when the hiring manager tells you they would like to offer you the job. This will set the tone for what follows. As a manager, calling someone and offering them the job is the prize for having to sit through a gruelling day of interviews, then having to call all the people who haven't been successful. Usually it is a positive, uplifting moment when the other person can't hide their excitement, which makes the hiring manager feel great and reaffirms the decision to select this candidate. However, when the person being offered the job has a lukewarm response at best, it is massively deflating. The hiring manager might start to wonder if the chosen candidate is the right person for the job.

2. **Stay professional.** As point 1 alluded to, the way you behave during a negotiation can have a significant impact on the outcome. Every so often I come across a Jekyll and Hyde candidate. During the recruitment process they are polite and professional, saying all the right things and creating the impression of someone who would be a perfect fit for the team. However, the moment they are offered the job, they undergo some sort of transformation, revealing a side of themselves that they had done well to hide during the interview process. Often this includes a lack of gratitude (giving the impression that they would be doing the hiring manager a huge favour by coming to work for them), making unreasonable demands, and being impossible to

contact to discuss if they are planning to accept the offer or not.

Please note: how much a hiring manager likes you is one of the most important factors in a negotiation. The more the manager wants you to come and work for them, the more they are likely to be willing to concede in order to get you on board. Judging the situation badly can be significantly costly. Remember, at this point all you have is a verbal, conditional offer, which can be withdrawn at any moment.

3. Take some time. You should never feel pressured into either negotiating or accepting a job straight away, over the phone. If you want some time to consider an offer and discuss it with friends and family then do so. Ask if you can call the hiring manager back the following day once you have spoken to your significant other (or whomever you speak to in these situations). However, be careful not to push your luck here. Unless it is over a weekend, I always feel uneasy if someone asks for any more than a day.

4. Be honest. You've probably heard people talk about "win–win" situations when it comes to negotiation. I would define this as a point when a transaction can take place (in this case, the acceptance of a job offer) where both parties have had their key criteria for the deal met. In business school, they also teach you that a negotiation is a transaction that often has information asymmetry. This is defined as transactions where one party has more or better information than the other. In the case of a job negotiation, you know what you are willing to accept and what your priorities are (your information), and the hiring manager knows what they are able to offer you (their information). However, you start off blind as to the other person's information. This information asymmetry often leads to misunderstanding, tension, and failed offers.

People often think that you need to be highly guarded in a negotiation, not showing your hand for fear of losing your advantage, and to some extent this is true. However, the less you are willing to share with the hiring manager about what you want, the harder it will be to find a compromise that both sides are happy with. If there is a specific criterion that is your top priority and you are not willing to compromise on it, be honest and make that clear. People often hide behind salary, when in fact it is another factor that they are really concerned about.

I was speaking to a colleague recently who had just failed to negotiate an offer with someone who was moving from another department within her organisation. My friend, let's call her Susan, had made an initial offer, which the person had politely declined, providing no feedback or counter offer. Susan then increased the salary being offered, but again was rebuffed with no useful feedback, just a view that the candidate couldn't accept the offer as it didn't meet her needs. This went on until eventually the offer was withdrawn, leaving Susan with the impression that this candidate was only interested in money and had unrealistic expectations of her earning potential. A few weeks later Susan ran into the candidate's line manager at a training event (we'll call him Bob), who expressed surprise that he still had his member of staff. Susan explained that she could not pay the level of salary that the person seemed to want and so unfortunately she had to withdraw the offer and approach the second-choice candidate who gratefully accepted the job. Bob, looked rather shocked at the story, and explained that the candidate was one of the least money-oriented people he knew, and that the reason she had given for not accepting the offer was that she wanted to work four days a week. This came as rather frustrating news to Susan as a) she would have happily considered the post being four days a week, and b) at no point did the candidate mention this during the negotiation.

I think we can describe the situation above as a "lose–lose" outcome. Hiring managers are not mind readers, and so it is down to you to make it clear if there are specific things that you need in order to accept the job. I genuinely believe you have far more to gain by being honest than you have to lose.

5. Don't be greedy or play games. Once you have received an offer that meets the "win–win" criteria (i.e. you would be happy to accept it, and by the fact that the employer has made the offer, they are happy with it) you have a decision to make. As the criteria and priorities you set earlier have been met, common sense says you should gratefully accept the offer. However, there is always the temptation to continue to negotiate to see what else you can get.

I'm not going to say that you shouldn't do this as your aim should be to get the best deal you can. However, it is important that you understand and consider the risks associated with this. It is possible to turn a "win–win" into a "lose–lose" with aggressive or speculative negotiation. It is easy to think that you've got an acceptable offer on the table, and the worst that can happen is that you fail to negotiate a better deal and end up accepting that offer. While this may be true, what you may do is damage your relationship with your future boss by making unreasonable demands, which put them in a difficult position. Always stay conscious of

how your ongoing negotiations are affecting that relationship.

What I would never advise anyone to do is to start making
unsubstantiated claims, telling lies or playing games during
an employment negotiation. In other situations where you
may negotiate, such as buying a car, the rules are somewhat
different. People may play one dealer off against another (or
create a fictitious dealer who is offering them a great deal),
say that they couldn't possibly pay a price that they later
come back to and accept, or pretend to walk away in the
hope of making the dealer sweat for a few days. There are a
number of reasons why a negotiation such as purchasing a
car is very different to accepting a job offer, but the most
important two are as follows:

i) **Supply and demand.** Unless you are buying a top-end or
very rare vehicle, you tend to have a number of options of
where to buy your car from. As a result, if a negotiation
turns sour you know you can walk away and look elsewhere.
For most people, they don't have the luxury of multiple job
offers at the same time and so lack a backup option (William
Ury and Roger Fisher define this as a BATNA in their book
Getting to Yes, which stands for Best Alternative to a Negoti-
ated Agreement). A lack of a backup option means the
downsides of a poor negotiation are a lot higher.

ii) **Ongoing relationship.** For most of us, buying a car is
something we do once every few years at most. As a result,
people don't tend to have a close ongoing relationship with
the people at their local car dealership. Contrast this with
the relationship you are likely to have with your new
manager, whom you will probably see almost every day, and
to some extent be dependent on for your livelihood.

In my experience it is rare that people get two job offers at exactly the same time and are able to play one potential employer off against another (this probably happens far more in the commercial sector). Therefore, when someone tells me they have a competing offer and are being dazzled by what the other organisation is offering, I am always a little suspicious. My reaction to this situation is always the same (regardless of if I think the offer is real or fake). I tell them that I want people to work for me because they believe in what we are doing and genuinely want to be part of our team. Therefore, before they get too caught up in thinking about money or other benefits, they should take some time to think about which of the two organisations they really want to work for. Which is the best fit for them? Then I agree a time with them for them to get back to me with their thoughts. This avoids getting into a bidding war and usually results in a conclusion pretty quickly (especially if the alternative job is non-existent).

When to Hand in Your Notice

You should never hand in your notice to your existing employer while only holding a conditional offer, as at this point you have no guarantee of a job. I also advise people to go one step further and not tell anyone that they don't have to that they have received a conditional offer. On a number of occasions I have witnessed people receiving a conditional offer and delighting in telling everyone that they will be leaving, how great their new job is going to be (and how life will be so much better with their new employer), only to have the offer withdrawn for some reason. The result isn't just embarrassment, but it can harm your relationship with your current employer and colleagues.

Obviously getting a job offer is hugely exciting, and so it is natural to want to tell people, but I would suggest just telling trusted friends and family until you have an unconditional offer.

The exception to the "not telling anyone rule" is the people you have put down as referees, and your line manager (who will almost always be one of your referees). If you haven't spoken to these people prior to the interview, then now is the time to do so. As I said in Chapter 7, from a manager's perspective, there are few things worse than getting a reference request that you are not expecting. Therefore, it is vital that you let your referees know that you have been made a conditional offer, and that the company will be contacting them for a reference.

Chapter Summary

Let's review the key points we have covered in this chapter.

- There are two main types of job offer: conditional and unconditional.
- A conditional job offer is made first, and is an offer dependent on you meeting a number of criteria. The most common conditions are reference checks, background checks or proof of qualifications, but there can be a range of other criteria depending on the job.
- An unconditional offer is made once all the criteria listed as part of the conditional offer have been met.
- When negotiating a job offer, it is important to be clear on what you are willing to accept and what your priorities are before you start to negotiate.

- It is also important to understand the position of the person you are negotiating with. Depending on the organisation and industry sector of the job, the hiring manager may have limited ability to negotiate on certain things. The classic example is someone trying to negotiate for a higher salary, when the organisation they are negotiating with has a rigid pay structure.

- Job negotiations usually happen before a conditional offer has been made, so remember that the offer can be withdrawn at any point. Therefore, it is important that you stay professional and positive throughout the negotiation.

- Deciding to accept a job offer is a big decision and not one that should be rushed. It is perfectly acceptable to ask for some time (usually 24 hours at most) to speak to your family or significant other to make sure you are making the right decision.

- The best policy during a negotiation is honesty. If there are things that are really important to you, make sure the person you are negotiating with understands this. Playing games or lying to the hiring manager to try and get a better deal rarely works and risks damaging your future relationship.

- It is important to remember that conditional offers can easily be withdrawn by the employer, so never hand your notice in until you have a formal unconditional offer.

21

POST-INTERVIEW FEEDBACK

S o, we've talked about what to do when you get the call with an offer of a job. I sincerely believe that after reading this book, and applying what you've learned, you should have significantly increased your chances of getting that call. However, as we have discussed in Chapter 18, even when you do everything right, there are a whole host of reasons why you still might not get the job. Therefore, I think it is important to dedicate some time to thinking about how you handle the "not getting a job offer" call (otherwise known as rejection).

When making this call, many hiring managers like to engage in some feedback before breaking the bad news, almost as if they're trying to avoid the inevitable. This usually goes along the following lines: "You gave a really good interview and it was great to meet you. The panel was particularly impressed with your enthusiasm and knowledge and we especially liked the slide in your presentation about the sandcastle building – you clearly have a really good understanding of how that relates to the work we do here. We had a really strong field of candidates today and it was a very difficult decision for us to make, I can honestly say that it is rare to have so many evenly matched candidates, but unfortunately we've made the decision to appoint someone else."

I try to avoid doing this as all the person really wants to know is if they've got the job and it just seems cruel to leave them in suspense. I usually just thank them for taking the time to come to the interview and then give them the bad news. Once I've let them know, I then give a brief bit of feedback, but in my experience, people tend not to hear much beyond "you haven't got the job". I then ask if they would like further feedback, and if so offer to do that now or set up a time in a few days for another call. I much prefer the second option as it gives people a chance to absorb and come to terms with the news.

The Magic of Feedback

Getting feedback on why you didn't get a job is hard and usually not much fun to listen to. However, it is also a fantastic learning opportunity. As the classic quote, often attributed to Henry Ford, says, "If you always do what you've always done, you'll always get what you've always got." Therefore, if you want to improve your chances of succeeding next time round, you need to have some insight into why things didn't go your way this time, and that means getting feedback.

As a recruiting manager, giving feedback is a difficult game to play. People tend to receive feedback in one of three ways, which I refer to as the three mindsets.

1. The hear but don't listen mindset. This is the case for a lot of people, especially those who are given feedback straight after they have been told they haven't got the job. When people find out they haven't been successful, most will have a mixture of emotions, commonly embarrassment, disappointment, anger, frustration and confusion (if they thought they'd done well). It is like being punched in the stomach, and like most people who have been punched in the stomach, they are not overly receptive to some constructive feedback about how not to get punched in the stomach in the future. However, the vast majority of people are kind and polite, so rather than saying "no thanks", they will sit and listen to the feedback, but their minds will be elsewhere. My guess is most people would have trouble accurately recounting the feedback they received an hour after the conversation. This is why I offer people the opportunity to get some feedback at a later date, when they are more likely to absorb the information.

2. The hear and challenge mindset. These are the type of people that recruiting managers dread. Like the "hear but don't listen" group, they suffer a mix of emotions, but instead of zoning out and not really engaging with the feedback, they decide to fight. People who fall into this category are often individuals who were highly confident and thought the job was theirs, and as a result are far more embarrassed than other candidates. When they receive feedback, they tend to focus on specific comments such as "we felt you didn't have enough experience to lead a team of this size", and retort with questions about the successful candidate's experience, arguments about how they weren't given the opportunity to share enough about previous teams they had managed or retelling of their management credentials.

This kind of response to feedback is pointless and self-defeating for two reasons. Firstly, as mentioned above, getting clear honest feedback about why you didn't get a job is invaluable if you want to try and improve your chances of getting a job in the future. By being challenging and confrontational, you will likely stop the recruiting manager from giving you honest feedback. Instead they will resort to giving you benign, unhelpful feedback that is less likely to upset you. For example, "The panel thought you were brilliant, a really strong candidate, and on any other day you would have got the job; however, you came up against a candidate who has been doing this exact job at another organisation and so is a perfect fit for us." This kind of feedback will make a person feel a bit better about themselves, easing the pain in the short term, but will leave the candidate with the impression that there was nothing they could have done better, and they were just unlucky on this occasion.

Secondly, you are never going to change someone's mind. I have never heard of a situation when a hiring manager has rung up a candidate who was deemed un-appointable to tell them they haven't got the job, and the candidate has managed to convince the manager to change their mind, call the candidate who they have offered the job to and retract the offer, and then give the job to the (formerly) un-appointable candidate. I'm sure someone somewhere will claim that they have in fact pulled off this magic trick, but I'm not sure I'd believe them.

The far more common scenario is when an interview panel

has decided not to give someone a job, for good reason, but thought a lot of the candidate and think they might be better suited to other opportunities they will have in the near future. The hiring manager has made contact with them to break the bad news and give some feedback, and the individual has gone into full "hear and challenge" mode. At this point the manager sees a whole new side to the person. As a hiring manager, when this happens you feel massively relieved that you didn't offer this candidate the job and make a note not to hire this person in the future.

I experienced this recently with two people applying for a very senior role. We decided not to appoint as the panel felt that neither of the candidates were quite right for the role. One candidate took the news well, asked for as much feedback as he could get, and expressed his gratitude at being given the opportunity to interview for the post. The other candidate reacted badly, not being open to feedback and sending long, vitriolic emails to the panel members late at night. Guess which of the two I am more likely to hire in the future!

3. The listen and understand mindset. You won't be surprised to know that this is the category I believe everyone should fall into. If you genuinely want to listen, understand and, most importantly, learn, then it should become your task to get as much useful information as you can from the hiring manager (and possibly other panel members, but more on this later).

In order to extract all the information you can from the person giving you feedback, you first need to put them at ease. I realise that sounds odd, but let me explain. When a hiring manager picks up the phone to call a candidate, they never know which type of mindset they are going to get (hear but don't listen, hear and challenge, or listen and understand). The hiring manager might have an idea from the way the candidate performed at interview, but people are often putting on a show during an interview and the minute that veil drops, a whole new side to them is revealed. Because of this, most managers will approach the feedback with a level of caution, for fear of giving some very honest feedback to someone who turns out to be in the "hear and challenge" category and ending up being stuck on the phone with someone who is determined to argue on every point for an hour. Thus, you need to demonstrate to the person giving you feedback that you are not a member of team "hear and challenge", but rather a fully committed member of the "listen and understand" group. This can be done very simply by your response to the question "Would you like me to give you some feedback?" If your response is something along the lines of "Yes, that would be great. Anything you can tell me that would help me improve for the future would be greatly appreciated", then it sends a clear signal that you are going to take feedback graciously. Asking genuine questions in response to feedback is another surefire way of indicating you are someone open to honest critique. For instance, if the manager says "we liked your presentation, but felt that you didn't go into enough depth in certain areas", you could follow up by saying, "Yes, I found it very challenging to get everything I wanted to say into the ten minutes, do you think I would have been better covering fewer topic areas but going into more depth for each one?" As the feedback session goes on, the trust between the manager and the candidate builds, and this creates an environment when the candidate can genuinely learn how to improve.

How to Receive Feedback

Below are my top tips for receiving feedback. I can't stress enough that this is one of the best opportunities you will have to learn and improve. Don't waste it.

1. Try to separate the breaking of bad news from the feedback. Getting feedback can be a whirlwind experience, especially if it directly follows being told you haven't got the job. As I talked about earlier, most people struggle to absorb much of what is said to them and accept the feedback more out of politeness than anything else. That is why I always offer candidates who want feedback the opportunity to either receive it straight away or to arrange a follow-up call or meeting. I believe that receiving your feedback at a different time, once you have had the opportunity to come to terms with the fact you haven't got the job and have had a chance to deal with any anger or embarrassment you are feeling, is a far more productive way to work.

Hopefully as you read the previous section on the three types of mindsets people have when they receive feedback, you will be clearly of the view that you would like to be in the "listen and understand" group. However, that is often a conscious choice that goes out the window when the emotional side of our brain takes over from the logical side when receiving bad news. Therefore, separating the two events gives you the opportunity to reset your mindset and make the most of the opportunity to learn for the future.

If you are not given this option by the hiring manager, then it is perfectly reasonable to ask for it. When asked if you would like some feedback, if you respond with, "I would really appreciate the opportunity to get some feedback.

However, I'm not sure my mindset is right to properly listen just now so would it be possible to arrange a quick call with you later in the week?", I believe that most reasonable managers will agree to this (and be impressed that you have the level of emotional intelligence to realise that this isn't the best time for you to receive the feedback and have the guts to say so).

2. Make sure your mindset is right. As discussed above, people react to job feedback in a number of ways. You will likely only get one opportunity at receiving feedback from a hiring manager, so making sure you have the right mindset to do so (the "listen and understand" mindset) is vital. As you will see in point 1, the best way to do this is to separate getting the bad news from the feedback; however, this is not always possible. Therefore, just as you need to prepare yourself mentally to receive and negotiate a job offer, you equally need to be mentally ready to receive constructive feedback.

The key thing to remember is that despite how it may feel at the time, it isn't a personal issue between you and the hiring manager. A decision has been made and nothing you are going to say or do is going to change that.

3. Write things down. As always in life, people tend to hear what they want to hear. This is especially true when people are receiving a personal critique that involves some focus on the negatives. On a number of occasions, I have provided feedback to unsuccessful candidates who have applied for another position with me in the months that followed the initial interview. Some of these candidates showed that they had clearly taken my feedback on board while others repeated the same mistakes they made the first time round. I believe the level of feedback I give to people is pretty consistent; however, when I talk to these candidates, the difference seems to be in their memory of the feedback I have provided.

The best way to avoid placing your own bias on the feedback you receive is to write down what the person who is giving you feedback actually says, rather than your interpretation of what they say. The best way to do this is to take notes in real time. Don't wait for the conversation to be over, make a cup of tea, watch TV and then at some point in the future write down some notes, as while you will have been busy on other activities, your brain will have been busy concocting its own version of events. It is perfectly acceptable to say to the person who is giving you feedback, "Can you bear with me as I want to take notes as we talk so I can learn as much as possible from your feedback?" The example feedback form at the end of the chapter shows an easy way to record the feedback you get. A blank copy of this form is available to download at www.howtogethired.co.uk in the documents section.

4. Meet in person if you can. The vast majority of the time feedback will be given to candidates over the phone. However, some managers will offer to do it in person, especially for internal candidates within an organisation. If you're given this opportunity, grab it with both hands. Sitting down with someone face-to-face probably means that you are going to get 30 minutes of their time as opposed to five. This shows that this person feels you are worth investing their time in, which in turn shows that they may be interested in hiring you in the future. A face-to-face meeting with someone who is going to give you honest feedback is essentially career coaching, something people pay a lot of money for, and it can be yours for the price of a cup of coffee.

5. Get as much feedback as possible. When most people are interviewed for a job, they are interviewed by more than one individual. The more senior the job, the more people will likely be involved in the process (to the point where you may end up going through four or five stages of interview). Yet it is almost always the case that you are provided feedback from one person. This makes perfect sense from the panel's point of view, as it is the most efficient way of doing it, and means that the person gets one consistent message (as opposed to where two or more people give feedback which may differ). However, it does mean that you miss out on the opportunity to get valuable feedback from all those other people.

Therefore, if possible, you should see if you are able to speak to more than one person on the panel. Asking to do this is likely to strike fear into the heart of the hiring manager, so it is important that you do it in the correct way. If you ask too early, the hiring manager will likely think that you are going to be a difficult individual, possibly a "hear and challenge" type of person, who might try and use any difference in the feedback they receive as a reason to say the recruitment process was unfair. Therefore, you have to establish yourself as someone fully in the "listen and understand" camp before you broach the subject with the hiring manager. At this point they will hopefully appreciate that you are just eager to see where you went wrong so you can learn and develop, and therefore be more amenable to your request.

6. Don't limit feedback to the interview. Because the interview is usually the last stage of the process, most managers only offer feedback on that part of the process. This means that people rarely, if ever, get feedback on their job applications (usually if you don't make it through to interview you will not receive any feedback as to why you haven't been selected). This means that it is incredibly hard for people to improve their job application skills as the only feedback is binary (either you get an interview or you don't). But there is nothing to say that the feedback you get after an interview has to be limited to the interview. I encourage people to ask the hiring manager for feedback on their application as well. Just because you got through to the interview stage doesn't mean your application was perfect; for all you know, you might have just scraped through as another candidate dropped out. Use the opportunity to get feedback on your CV, application form, cover letter etc. It can't hurt to ask and you may be surprised by what you find out.

7. Don't be scared to ask questions. The reality for most hiring managers is that they will probably have a long list of people they need to call to break the news that they haven't got the job, and give feedback to those who want it. Therefore, their aim will be to get through the list as quickly and painlessly as possible. This means giving people an acceptable level of feedback but not taking more time than is required.

If you want to get some really useful feedback you can actually learn from, you may have to ask some questions rather than simply accepting what the hiring manager tells you. These could either be follow-up questions to their comments, for example "You mentioned that my slides were hard to follow, was it the design of the slides or the structure of the presentation (or both)?" or a question about an area that they haven't covered, for example "I felt like I could have answered the scenario questions a bit better, especially the one about dealing with change, can you give me some feedback on how I did?"

This may feel slightly awkward, but it is important to remember that during this conversation you are actually in a more powerful position than you might think. Yes, the hiring manager is the person who makes the decision about whether or not you get hired, but by this point that decision is made. From a manager's perspective, having these conversations is hard, and they will (usually) feel genuine sympathy for the candidate. Therefore, if the candidate asks something of the manager, the manager will generally feel compelled to try and help (within reason). Most managers I have spoken to have said they would happily answer specific questions from candidates, so long as they're happy that they are not speaking to someone who is likely to be challenging.

8. Take time to reflect. The final mistake many people make is doing some or all of steps 1 to 7 above, but then not taking the time to reflect on what they have learned. Remember the Stephen Covey quote from earlier in the book: "to know and not to do is really not to know". Once you have amassed this valuable feedback, you need to turn it into some clear actions you can take to improve your chances for next time. As I mentioned at the end of step 3, there is a blank copy of the feedback form shown below available to download at www.howtogethired.co.uk in the documents section. This form serves two purposes. Firstly, it provides somewhere for you to write down the feedback you get in a structured way. This is split into two main parts:

"things I did well" and "areas for improvement". Both are equally important. Most people will focus on the things they got wrong during an interview and not take much notice of the positive feedback they receive.

The second purpose is to give you an opportunity to write down how you plan to build on your strengths and address your weaknesses in the future. The right-hand column asks you to write down what you can do to improve in the future. The example feedback from below shows how this may look.

	Feedback	What can I do to improve?
Things I did well		
1.	They felt I had done my research on the company and clearly understood the requirements of the job.	Write down a list of the steps I went through in researching the company this time so I can use it as a guide when I next apply for a job.
2.	Seemed very approachable and showed good communication skills.	Keep doing this. Remember to try and make contact with the recruiting manager prior to the interview next time.
Areas for improvement		
1.	Multiple spelling mistakes on my application form.	Get someone else to proofread my application.
2.	Panel felt my presentation was muddled and seemed to jump about a lot. It made it hard to follow the logic behind my recommendation.	Spend more time planning my presentations to ensure that there is a clear structure in place. Use a summary or conclusion slide at the end to make sure my key points are clear. Rehearse my presentation to people to get some feedback on whether it flows.
3.	Although I have a lot of experience in HR the job went to a candidate that had a formal HR qualification.	Investigate what HR qualifications are available and the money and time commitment required. See if this is something my current employer would fund.

This document can form the start of a checklist that you can refer to as you build up your experience. Writing down the things that you know you've done well, your areas for improvement and the actions you've taken helps to track your personal development. This in turn will help to build your confidence. If every time you apply for a job or attend an interview you take away three positives and three things you can improve, and add them to your list, whether you get the job or not, you will quickly build up a level of personal insight that will set you apart from 99% of the candidates out there.

Chapter Summary

Let's review the key points we have covered in this chapter.

- If you have not been successful in getting the job, it is important to learn as much as you can so you can improve for the future. Getting feedback isn't much fun, but it is a huge opportunity to learn.
- People tend to react in one of three ways when receiving feedback: the "hear but don't listen" mindset, where the person doesn't absorb much after being told they haven't got the job; the "hear and challenge" mindset, where people become very defensive and try to challenge the recruiting manager's points rather than accepting them; and the "listen and understand" mindset, where people accept that they haven't been successful on this occasion and use the opportunity to learn as much as they can for the future.
- There are a number of steps you can take to ensure you get the maximum benefit from the feedback you are offered:

- Try to separate getting the bad news from receiving the feedback if possible.
- Make sure your mindset is right before you speak to the person giving you feedback.
- Try to make notes as you receive the feedback as it is important to write down what was actually said, not your interpretation of the feedback.
- Meet the person face-to-face if possible as you will get much more feedback this way.
- Get feedback from as many people as possible.
- Don't limit the feedback you get to your interview. Ask how your application could have been stronger.
- Don't be scared to ask questions of the person giving you feedback.
- Take the time to reflect on the feedback you are given.

22

THANK YOU AND GOOD LUCK

We have now reached the end of our journey and I hope it has been a useful one. I want to take this opportunity to thank you for buying this book and taking the time to read it. I truly believe that if you put into practice what you have learned, you can and will find the job of your dreams. By the very fact that you have gone to the effort of buying a book to help you in this process, you have put yourself ahead of most of the people you will be competing with for your dream job.

As I said at the start of the book, the key skills needed to win in the recruitment process are all skills that can be learned and perfected with practice. This book can help you to learn them, but only you can do the practice.

I hope this book will become a valuable tool that can support you throughout your career, and you can share what you have learned with others who need the support. I would love to hear your thoughts, comments and feedback, which you can send to me via the book's website (www.howtogethired.co.uk)   or   e-mail   me   at howtogethiredinfo@gmail.com.

All that is left for me to do is to thank you, wish you good luck and ask that if you have enjoyed this book and found it helpful, please give it a quick review on Amazon, as reader feedback is so important in reaching new readers.

Take care

Mike Harrison